abe • bad version • bambino • bando • blow up • **boffo** •
book • bootie record • box office • call sheet • cattle call
cha cha cha • chantoosie • ciao • **chopsocky** • churban •
cock rock • craft • craft service • cut to the chase • deal m
evelopment hell • DOA • drop • doughboy • films • flack
e) flashing • go-see • goebbles • got ears • green room • gr
loor rewrite • **helmer** • hickey • **high concept** • high schm
hit the streets • Hollywood • Hollywood heartbeat • horse b
hyphenate • in the can • indie • indier than thou • Industry
jackets • jam • **japananimation** • juice • logline • (to le
MAW • meatpuppet • ntbslt • offish • Oscar • Oscar nod •
ner • Pasadena • peeled • pen • pitch • player • playola •
press whore • **product** • punch it up • Q • roll calls • san
chmooze • shamefest • show • Sillywood • skeezer • sour
star baggage • starrer • stretch • suit • talking head • tight
nt • (to throw a) Rudin • toast • **track** • trackers • trades •
round • **vanilla extract** • vanity show • wank trade • we
wheel • white label • with a bullet • with an anchor • **wrap** •
arty • against the law • Amazon • Ann O'Rexia • b-boys • bad
Baldwin • Barney • betty • beard • beast • **beer gogg**
ee-yotch • bell hop • bender • **biddy** • biff • bim • bitch •
nagnet • bod squad • boxmaster • bomber • bootie call • l
reakdown • breeders • buffy • buppie • **cave bitch** • cha
heese kransky • chip trip • clock • clowns • cock block •
cradle robber • creep • dahmer • deeko • **dexter** • dick •
ss wonder • dingleberry • doable • dog • double bagger • d
oy • dork • dude • **dump the chump** • de facto • faggot
ag • **farley** • fatzilla • filth • filthy • fine • fishing fleet •
hicks • flock • fly girl • fox • freak • fugly • **full moon** • ga
y • gal pal • **gaydar** • gettin' any? • good to his mom • go
got it going on • got skills • **granola** • halfing • hands off
o toe • helen keller • hen party • high maintenance • himbo • h
oy/girl • homey clown • honey • **honey dripper** • hoodie • l
at • hook in • **horkle** • hot ticket • hottie • in the club • l
jettison cargo • keeper • kick the ballistics • kleenex • laven
e and fleas • load • lowball • **mack daddy** • mack • ma
ickle • mad bitches • main squeeze • meat market • miss th
onet • mosquito bites • mudflaps • nasty • nasty lass • **nel**
mrod • no-neck • **o-beast** • O.P.P. • our team • pash • p
ercy bird • P.I.C. • pizza face • player • poindexter • poz •
no-babe • pugly • puppies • **quimby** • ragamuffin • raspy •
rocker • saucalicious • scab • scam • scene • **schwing** • sce
loot the gift • skank • skeezer • sketch • smooth daddy • sn
oap on a rope • space vixen • spade a chick • spliced • spur
squallie • square john • **squid** • stallion • star fucker • steady
step out • stunts • sweetie • tard • tasty • **tenderoni** • t
er thighs • tire kicker • **tomato** • trailer trash • tranzie • tr
vo-bagger • umpa loompa • vacuumed • wang • walker • wl
iit • wigger • wilma • **winnie bago** • woman years • wus
ahoo • yorkel • zootie • advertiser • beater • bed dancer • be
bike dyke • bird dog • blew-it • boney • **booted** • braille • l
icket • broadie • **bust a left** • buy-n-die • caddie • Californi
cancer • candied • cashmere • cherry • croakwago
otchrocket • cruiser • derogs • detail • ding • dust 'em • fa

BUZZ WORDS

a buzz book

L.A. Fresh Speak

**Anna Scotti and
Paul Young**

st. martin's press • new york

Web Site: http://www.buzzmag.com

Production Editor: David Stanford Burr

Book Design by Gretchen Achilles

Library of Congress Cataloging-in-Publication Data

Scotti, Anna.
     Buzzwords / by Anna Scotti and Paul Young.—
1st ed.
                 p.   cm.
     "A Buzz book."
     ISBN 0-312-15488-7
     1. English language—California—Los Angeles—
Slang—Dictionaries.   2. Americanism—California—
Los Angeles—Dictionaries.   3. Los Angeles (Calif.)—
Languages—Dictionaries.   I. Young, Paul D.
II. Title.
PE3101.C3S36   1997
427'.979494'03—dc21
                                  96-40423
                                  CIP

First Buzz Book Edition: May 1997

10 9 8 7 6 5 4 3 2 1

Table of Contents

Acknowledgments

Special thanks go out to Tony Baumeister and his crew for some amazing skater speak, Wikid and A.K., better known as the rap group Juvenile Style for the dope Eastside shit, photographer Reggie Casagrande for her outrageous X-rated street jargon, fashion maven April Sassick for the hip garmento stuff, doorman extraordinaire Eric Lorenz for *the chiz* on L.A. nightlife lingo, electric bass legend Mike Watt for the *Pedro* slang, Channon Roe for his killer surferese, and Seth "Raggs" Adams who, just by virtue of being the best *smack magnet* on the West Coast, always has the latest and greatest without even trying.

Other valued contributions came from Cherish Alexander, Jordan Alan, Scott Birkson, Vickie Brinkord, Laura Connelly, Jim "the Mad Monk" Crotty, Jaime Glantz, Eric Knorr, Tanya Pampalone, Kendall Swanson, Sydney Zekley, and the hundreds of *hipsters, horkles,* and *hoes* everywhere.

—PAUL YOUNG

Thanks and big ups to Peter Barsocchini, Alix Clarke, Ann Flower, Diana Foutz, Linda Friedman, Susan Gordon, Katy Harris, Bob Makela, Ken Neville, Nadine Ono, Anthea Orlando, Lisa Simpson, Nina Wiener, to Eden Collinsworth for a great idea, to our editor, Jim Fitzgerald, to all those anonymous donors, witting and unwitting, to my husband, and lots of kisses to Victoria, who didn't help much, but who deserves them all the same.

—ANNA SCOTTI

abe • bad version • bambino • bando • blow up • **boffo** •
book • bootie record • box office • call sheet • cattle call •
ha cha cha • chantoosie • ciao • **chopsocky** • churban •
cock rock • craft • craft service • cut to the chase • deal me
evelopment hell • DOA • drop • doughboy • films • flack
e) flashing • go-see • goebbles • got ears • green room • gr
oor rewrite • **helmer** • hickey • **high concept** • high **schm**
hit the streets • Hollywood • Hollywood heartbeat • horse bl
hyphenate • in the can • indie • indier than thou • Industry
jackets • jam • **japananimation** • juice • logline • (to le
AW • meatpuppet • ntbslt • offish • Oscar • Oscar nod •
ner • Pasadena • peeled • pen • pitch • player • playola •
press whore • **product** • punch it up • Q • roll calls • sam
hmooze • shamefest • show • Sillywood • skeezer • soun
star baggage • starrer • stretch • suit • talking head • tight
nt • (to throw a) Rudin • toast • **track** • trackers • trades •
ound • **vanilla extract** • vanity show • wank trade • wet
wheel • white label • with a bullet • with an anchor • **wrap** •
rty • against the law • Amazon • Ann O'Rexia • b-boys • bad
Baldwin • Barney • betty • beard • beast • **beer goggl**
e-yotch • bell hop • bender • **biddy** • biff • bim • bitch •
agnet • bod squad • boxmaster • bomber • bootie call • B
eakdown • breeders • buffy • buppie • **cave bitch** • char
eese kransky • chip trip • clock • clowns • cock block • c
cradle robber • creep • dahmer • deeko • **dexter** • dick •
ss wonder • dingleberry • doable • dog • double bagger • do
y • dork • dude • **dump the chump** • de facto • faggot •
g • **farley** • fatzilla • filth • filthy • fine • fishing fleet •
icks • flock • fly girl • fox • freak • fugly • **full moon** • gal
• gal pal • **gaydar** • gettin' any? • good to his mom • gor
got it going on • got skills • **granola** • halfing • hands off •
toe • helen keller • hen party • high maintenance • himbo • h
y/girl • homey clown • honey • **honey dripper** • hoodie • **h**
t • hook in • **horkle** • hot ticket • hottie • in the club • l
ettison cargo • keeper • kick the ballistics • kleenex • lavend
e and fleas • load • lowball • **mack daddy** • mack • mac
kle • mad bitches • main squeeze • meat market • miss thi
net • mosquito bites • mudflaps • nasty • nasty lass • **nell**
nrod • no-neck • **o-beast** • O.P.P. • our team • pash • pa
rcy bird • P.I.C. • pizza face • player • poindexter • poz •
o-babe • pugly • puppies • **quimby** • ragamuffin • raspy •
ocker • saucalicious • scab • scam • scene • **schwing** • sco
oot the gift • skank • skeezer • sketch • smooth daddy • sno
ap on a rope • space vixen • spade a chick • spliced • spun
quallie • square john • **squid** • stallion • star fucker • steady b
tep out • stunts • sweetie • tard • tasty • **tenderoni** • tl
thighs • tire kicker • **tomato** • trailer trash • tranzie • tro
o-bagger • umpa loompa • vacuumed • wang • walker • wh
t • wigger • wilma • **winnie bago** • woman years • wus
hoo • yorkel • zootie • advertiser • beater • bed dancer • bee
ike dyke • bird dog • blew-it • boney • **booted** • braille • b
ket • broadie • **bust a left** • buy-n-die • caddie • California
cancer • candied • cashmere • cherry • croakwagor
tchrocket • cruiser • darage • detail • dic

Preface

I love language. Call me a poet but I enjoy choosing the right word for the right occasion; I love the sound of newly minted slang. Love the booming and buzzing of our communal short-hand. The first slang word I ever grew fond of I heard in the third grade. I learned the snappy word, *neat*. I put it in to heavy rotation. I remember this so clearly because my mother was vehemently anti-slang. She gave me a lot of grief. "Why does everything have to be *neat*?" she would taunt me. "Why use *slang* when there are so many colorful, descriptive real words to choose from? For instance, *magnificent!* or *delight-ful!* or *fantastic!*?"

So I tried not to say *neat* in her presence. But of course, its forbidden status made that impossible. Plus I think I knew instinctively that to hear an eight year old repeatedly exclaim-ing "Magnificent!" or "Delightful" would be not just repulsive but borderline terrifying.

Today I exercise caution over what new slang I add to my everyday speech. Like, once you leave the school system it takes longer to find the proper casual-yet-in-the-know tone to use with new phrases. So I'm careful; one can look the fool in a millisecond, date oneself with one exclamation, even re-veal self-esteem issues with a stale retort. Choosing the wrong slang is a lot like wearing the wrong trendy outfit. You need a good, grounded sense of what you can pull off. No one is more judgmental about this sort of thing than I am. I'll write people off if they use a slang expression whose shelf life has expired. One little "been there, done that" or "I give good phone" and I tune out everything else that person says.

And another thing, I've never been comfortable with made-up words. I can't say "groovy" or "bitchin' " or even "rad" without feeling embarrassed. My favorite slang involves makeovers for your basic, quotidian words. In my opinion, *slangization* was the best thing that ever happened to "wicked," "heinous," and "bogus." This book gifted me uses for the common words: *core, brutal, spun,* and *random* that will conceivably worm their way in to my life, speech, and banter. I'll express myself better for it!

If in reading this book any of us adds one new phrase or word to our speech, well then . . . as long as we don't run into each other, we'll do just fine.

—MERRILL MARKOE

Introduction

Are you *tapped out* or *fat bank*? Would you be found *macking down* on a date or in front of the TV? If someone called you a *player*, would be you offended or pleased?

The choicest, *edgiest,* juiciest BUZZWORDS we collected originated in hip-hop and rap culture, with the film and music industries, surf and skate culture, and the beauty business all kicking in *big time,* too. Gangster slang of the thirties and forties *(busting chops),* 1960s counterculture lingo *(groovy, peace),* seventies *mush-speak* and eighties style power-prefixing have all resurfaced in L.A. of late, and the odd British, Australian, and South African expressions have somehow found their way into mainstream speech. Spanish and Spanglish are, of course, heavily represented, from *cojones* in the boardroom to the real *chiz* on the street.

We've avoided — often regretfully — terms that are particular only to a specific job or hobby *(slappy grind,* for a skateboard move, or *mini-mole* for a special light used on a movie set). This collection is comprised of words that have crossed over, fully or partially, into mainstream speech. Not every Angeleno knows what it means to *throw a Rudin* or to *scope a biddy,* but you don't have to be a film gaffer — or a *tire kicker* — to find out.

If there's a single identifiable trend happening in L.A. slang circa 1997, it's the cross-dressing of jargon: women can have *brass balls,* and men — even straight men — are sometimes *bitches.* With the colorful exception of some body-parts descriptions, you'll be hard-pressed to find many terms in this book that apply to one sex and not the other. Figuring out which word to use when is a little trickier — something like knowing which note to hit in a jazz improv session. For example, a nice car might be *slammin', sick, wicked, whack, out-of-control, sweet, phat, dope, illified, prada, bitchin', cherry, rad, trick, epic, monster, pimpy,* or just *way insane.* Use the wrong word in the wrong place at the wrong time and you'll *come off* like a *poser,* a *Barney,* a *wigger* — maybe even a *creepo suave.*

As a rule of thumb, the word that sounds best is the one to use—*phat ride* rolls off the tongue a little quicker than *whack ride,* and *that paint job is wicked* just sounds better than *that paint job is whacked.*

Then again, what's right and wrong? Hip-hop slang passes into beach culture and is soon appropriated by the Valley folk. The main thing to remember when speaking *Angeleno* is to relax, draw out your vowels, forget about raising your voice. You could try a little *upspeak*? It might help you *chill out*? If you're a local *smack magnet,* send us some words for the next edition. Otherwise, *kick back* and *peep it out.*

ANNA SCOTTI
c/o St. Martins Press,
Inc. 175 Fifth Avenue
New York, NY 10010

THE SCHMOOZEFEST

Angelyne, Ahnold, and Alan Smithee

Academy: The Academy of Motion Picture Arts and Sciences—the body that selects recipients of the *Oscar*.

Ahnold: universally recognized to mean Schwarzenneger.

Alan Smithee: pseudonym used by a director who doesn't want his name attached to a final project. Now used by or for anybody who has little or no interest in his work.

Angelyne: disparaging term for a self-promoter with more aspirations than talent, especially but not exclusively a creative or performing artist (after the ubiquitous billboard queen). Also, a *woodruff*.

(to be) attached: what a person is when he is signed to a film project before it is completely cast and crewed: "It's *in the bag*—we've got Scorsese *attached* as producer."

(to be) attached

babe: yep, movie people really say it.

bad version: how you describe *your* version of what you want a writer/actor/etc. to do: "The third act needs *punching up*—like Cliff drops dead and April has to pilot the jumbo jet blindfolded—that's the *bad version*."

bambino: Italian for child, often used faux-affectionately for adults. Similar to *babe, baby, you kids*. (Also see *cha cha cha*.)

bando: a music groupie.

(to) blow up: to get famous, popular, successful: "That song is *blowing up* (on) the charts!" Also, *to take off*.

boffo: horrible sixties adjective meaning *terrific* that has, improbably, made a comeback.

bomb: a box office loser. (Also see MORE SLAMS AND PROPS.) Also *to tank*.

book: 1.) a print model's portfolio. 2.) to land an acting role or modeling job. (Also see EVERYDAY LIFE.)

bootie record: A *jam* about *bootie*, or one that makes you want to shake your *bootie*—that is, a hit dance record.

box office: a synecdoche for box office receipts: "The movie sucks, but it's doing good *box office*."

buck sheet: that long, narrow card used for scribbling messages, usually *re* rejected scripts. The bigger the VIP, the less info the *buck sheet* contains—sometimes no address or phone, just a company logo.

(the) Business: the entertainment business, that is, film, television, and stage. Used by those in and out of it. Sometimes includes music, radio, modeling, and related fields. Also, the *Biz* and the *Industry*.

call sheet: 1. a list of phone calls to be returned. 2. the 411 on the next day's shoot.

cattle call: an open call audition or modeling *go-see*—that is, one to which many candidates have been invited.

(to) cha cha cha: to get going, to make something happen: "Messenger over that *deal memo, bambino,* and we'll *cha cha cha.*"

chantoosie: a female singer (from chanteuse).

chopsocky: industry term for a martial arts film.

churban: denotes the type of music played by radio stations that combine contemporary hit radio (CHR) with urban (Black) music.

ciao: good-bye. More sixties slang that's back in vogue.

cleffer: a songwriter.

cock rock: heavy metal rock and roll.

cock rock

(my) craft: how spacey actors refer to their profession: "I haven't worked in six years, but I've been practicing *my craft* by taking classes."

craft service: catering company that provides munchies on a film set. Some spillover to general usage.

cut to the chase: get to the action, get to the point.

deal memo: a written statement of intentions that precedes an actual written contract. Also used metaphorically.

development hell: an endless series of negotiations between *suits* and *talent*. See *turnaround*.

DOA: refers to a script that is out of the running *(dead on arrival)* before it's even read, usually because of amateurish touches like spiral binding or nonstandard format.

doughboy: caterer on a film set. (Also see THE MEET MARKET.)

drop: to become available, to *hit the streets*: "That record *drops* September fifteenth."

films: what movies are called in *Hollywood*. Also, *picture*.

flack: a publicist—usually a personal publicist, as opposed to one who handles noncelebrity clients. Also, a *praiser*.

(to be) flashing (green/yellow/red): describes the status of a project. If *green,* the project is a go or almost a go. If *yellow,* it's stalled, and if *red*—there are serious obstacles ahead: "Honey, I want to cast you in the lead, but we're *flashing yellow* until Steven meets with the investors."

gang-bang: a group-writing session for television. (Also see STREETLIFE.)

Goebbels: head of publicity at a studio or record label (yes, as in Joseph).

go-see: a modeling interview, a chance for a client to see whether a model is right for a particular job.

got ears: able to recognize songs that are potential hits.

green room: an area used by guests waiting to appear on a television show, so called because it is often painted green, or because its inhabitants often turn green with anxiety. (Also see STREETLIFE.)

ground-floor rewrite: what even a not-so-bad script usually gets.

helmer: film director (he or she is *at the helm*).

hickey: a favorable review. Less politely called a *blowjob*.

high concept: describes an idea so simple and commercially appealing that it can be expressed in a single sentence or even a single phrase: *Demi strips*. (Originally a film term, now crossing over to general usage.)

high schmooze: describes a function with an unusually high number of heavyweights in attendance. Also, *schmooze factor*, the ratio of VIPs to regular people at a particular event, *low schmooze* (not many), *schmoozability* (describes a person's receptivity to being *schmoozed*).

(to) hit the streets: to become available to the public— usually used about an album or video. (Also see *drop*.)

Hollywood: 1.) the *Industry*—not to be confused with the actual place, where most *Hollywood players* would not be caught dead. 2.) an affectionate moniker: "Yo, *Hollywood!*"

(in a) Hollywood heartbeat: an instant. Similar to a *New York Minute*.

horse blanket: camera technique used to soften an actor's face: "She's complaining about her wrinkles again— better throw a horse blanket on the lens." Sometimes used metaphorically.

hyphenate: a person with a hyphenated job title: writer-director, guitarist-singer. Also, *slash:* writer *slash* director.

in the can: originally referred to exposed reels of film *in the can,* now refers to the completion of any project in any field.

indie: independent, whether a radio station, film company, record label, producer, product, whatever. Note that even big budget projects can have—or try for—an *indie flavor.*

indier than than thou: describes a music group that professes to be underground or countercorporate: "Epitaph Records is so *indier than thou*—they swear they'll never sell out to a major."

Industry: 1.) *the Business*—that is, the entertainment business. 2.) of or pertaining to *the Business:* "if it's not an *Industry* party, I'm busy that night."

(to) ink: to sign a deal.

jackets: businessmen or business people. Implies square, straightlaced types as opposed to *artistes:* "Believe me, Julio, I'd write more perks into your contract, but I gotta answer to the *jackets.*" Also, *suits.*

jam: once a verb meaning to play music, now a noun meaning a hot music cut or a verb meaning to leave. Not to be confused with *jammy.* (See THE MEET MARKET.)

Japanamation: stylish, graphic, adult-oriented animation in TV shows and movies. Also, *anime* (pronounced an-e-may).

juice: power, *connections*: "You can't get past the front desk unless you've got some *juice*." (Seldom used by locals to refer to the notorious former sports star.)

(to) lens: to shoot a film.

locals: third-rate talent (especially models).

logline: originally a one-sentence description of a screenplay ("railroaded con gets pardon, seeks revenge") now used for a concise summation of any kind: "Skip all the *blah-blah* about your date last night, Jane, and just give me the *logline*."

MAW: model/actress/whatever. Often used disparagingly. Also, *wammie*.

meat puppet: 1.) an actor or spokesperson. 2.) a prostitute.

monster: the nineties term for blockbuster: "You can bet that with Spielberg on board, it'll be *monster*!"

name: a star or other recognizable person: "It's a good script, but we need a *name*."

ntbslt: not this, but something like this: "Act three is flat. We need the hero to—ntbslt—blow up the terrorist's island with the hijacked atom bomb." Same as the *bad version*.

offish: a little off, not performing to expectation: "that film's a little *offish* with female viewers."

Oscar: often, and annoyingly, written and spoken without an article: "Who will take home *Oscar*?" instead of, "who will take home *an Oscar*?" Also, *the god of tchotchkes*.

Oscar nod: an Academy Award nomination: "Over the years, her work has snagged three *Oscar nods,* but no win."

page oner: a screenplay that needs a *ground floor rewrite*.

(to) Pasadena: to pass on a script, that is, to reject it. Also used as an adjective: "It's *Pasadena*."

(to get) peeled: to go into overtime on a film set. (Also see THE BODY BEAUTIFUL.)

(to) pen: to write.

pitch: a proposal. Also, *to pitch*.

player: person of weight and importance in the *Industry*. This word has multiple, slightly related meanings. (Also see THE MEET MARKET, WORK, and STREETLIFE.)

playola: having employees or friends of artists call radio stations en masse to request airplay for specific songs, or calling a 900 number to request airplay from a pay-to-play video channel (from the bite-your-tongue term *payola* plus *play*).

(to) plug: to promote (as a record, book, or film).

press whore: a person, usually a celebrity or a self-styled expert, desperate for attention. Also, *press hound, press slut, press groupie*.

product: any film, record, or artwork, especially those produced for the general public.

(to) punch it up: to make a text or script more exciting: "The first act's a snooze—*punch up* the *wet stuff*."

Q: a measure of a celebrity's recognizability and likability for television. Also, *Q rating*.

(to) roll: to start, to bring on. See *talent*.

(to) roll calls: to have one's assistant set up a nonstop flow of calls from the *call sheet*, ranked by order of importance: "Courtney, I'm stuck on the *405! Roll calls!*"

sample: a sound sample—that is, a small portion of a recording that is used in another (usually rap or hip-hop) recording. Also, *bite, grab, steal*.

(to) schmooze: to do business under the guise of socializing, especially obsequiously.

shamefest: an *Industry* party where everyone is *schmoozing*.

show: a film in production—the preferred term that has largely replaced *picture*: "I've got a *show* in Montana, and another in Miami."

Sillywood: the CD-ROM industry (from *Silicon Valley* and *Hollywood*). Also, *Hollywired*.

sound bite: a single phrase or word pulled from an interview. Celebrities, hoping to be quoted, often speak in pithy *sound bites*.

stalkerazzi: aggressive freelance photographers.

star baggage: the money allocated, in a production budget, to accomodate the top star's personal perks.

starrer: a movie with a *name attached* to star: "a Sharon Stone *starrer.*"

stretch: a test of one's acting ability when one is cast against type. Often used sarcastically: "We'll cast him as the *himbo,* that'll be a *stretch.*"

suit: a disparaging term for record executives, used by promoters, djs, and artists. Also, any executive or any person who's *L7.*

talking head:
1.) a news anchor.
2.) a spokesperson.
3.) a very intelligent person. 4.) a movie shot for video — that is, one with too many close-ups.

tight: well written, without extraneous words and scenes. (Also see MORE SLAMS AND PROPS and EVERYDAY LIFE.)

suit

(to) take bows: to steal credit: "We got Miss Ross the comeback gig, but her *flacks* are *taking bows.*"

talent: Performers. Actors, models, musicians are *talent*; directors, screenwriters, and songwriters are (usually) not. Usually disparaging: "*Roll* the *talent*, I need a laugh."

(to throw a) Rudin: to have a tantrum (from the notoriously ill-tempered producer Scott Rudin).

track: a *jam*.

trackers: D-girls. That is, low-level film and television development executives of either sex.

trades: the magazines and newspapers particular to an industry, especially music and film.

turnaround: where a script goes when the studio that has optioned or purchased it declines to make it or to renew the option. The screenwriter is then free to sell the script again, which is why there are worse places to be than in *turnaround hell*.

vanilla extract: describes a high-profile celebrity who displays little personality or individuality: "He's *wild* about Whitney Houston, but she's *vanilla extract* to me." (Compare to *white bread*/EVERYDAY LIFE.) Also, *Saccharin*.

vanity show: a project put into development just to make a star happy: "Eastwood's set to direct the action flick, but first we have to okay his *vanity show*."

wank trade: the porno industry.

wet stuff: sex and/or violence (in a script).

wheel: a *player*, a VIP.

white label: refers to a record that is not signed to a record company, or is signed but for any of a variety of reasons is to be played on the radio anonymously (often because it includes *samples* that have not been cleared, or approved for use).

with a bullet: hot and happening, moving up the record charts. Opposite of the obsolete *with an anchor.*

(to) wrap: originally to finish a film or TV production, now to complete any project or encounter: "I'm not really dating Tom anymore—I think it's time to call it a *wrap.*"

wrap party: a celebration to mark a *wrap.*

THE MEET MARKET

Boy Meets Girl, Or Boy Meets Boy, Or Girl Meets . . .

against the law: more beautiful than should be allowed — suggests tough, cool, and a little dangerous.

Amazon: 1.) a tall shapely woman — used admiringly. 2.) a strong, powerful, or aggressive woman.

Ann O'Rexia: an exceptionally thin female.

asspro: male prostitute.

back: a rear end, specifically, a *full moon*. Often, *baby got back,* which is one of those odd expressions that can be either a *prop* or a *slam*.

bad cook: a widower.

bad hat: a pimp. Also, a *judas*.

Ann O'Rexia

Baldwin: a cute guy (as in Alec, Billy, and Stephen).

ball maul: a man-hating woman.

Barney: 1.) the opposite of a *Baldwin*. 2.) to bungle, to do something stupid. 3.) a novice. (Also see THE BODY BEAUTIFUL.)

b-boys: 1.) cool young guys (the *b* being *Black*). 2.) bar boys—those who like to party. Also, *b-girls*.

beard: 1.) the husband or wife of a homosexual who makes it possible for him or her to "pass" as straight. 2.) a woman who pretends to be a lesbian. (Also see THE BODY BEAUTIFUL.)

beast: an unattractive person of either gender.

beat sheets: pornographic material.

(to have) beaver fever: to be sex-crazed.

betty: disparaging, but somewhat affectionate, term for an attractive but dim-witted female. Also, *beach betty*.

beer goggles: what you wear, metaphorically, after a few drinks . . . and they tend to make everyone look pretty *doable*.

bee-yotch: 1.) originally a disparaging street term for women, rapidly appropriated by middle-aged *suits* forbidden by their wives to say *bitch*. 2.) an affectionate greeting between men: "*S' up, bee-yotch?*"

bell hop: a straightlaced, boring male.

bender: cross-dresser (from *gender bender*).

biddy: a female, often implies young and attractive.

biff: 1.) an athlete, a jock. 2.) a preppy male.

big willy: a penis. (Also see STREETLIFE.)

bim: a bimbo.

bitch: originally (and still) a disparaging term for women, but now often used by men, for men—something along the lines of *wussy*. Also used affectionately. (Also see *bee-yotch*.)

bitch magnet: a male who attracts females. Also *biddy magnet, fox magnet,* etc.

blow monkey: 1.) a person who gives fellatio. 2.) a person who snorts cocaine.

(to) boadwee: to have diarrhea or to defecate (from the artist notorious for squirting paint from his rectum).

bod squad: good-looking boys or girls traveling in a pack.

(to) boink: to have sex.

boo: one's girlfriend. (Also see THE WHEEL MEANING OF LIFE.)

bomber: a badly dressed person.

bootie: 1.) a person's rear end. 2.) set. 3.) any good stuff.

bootie call: a libidinous urge. (Also see THE SCHMOOZEFEST.)

BOT: bachelor over thirty. Sometimes implies gay, often pejorative.

boxmaster: man known or expected to be good in bed.

breakdown: a bad date: "Was it *fun?* We're talking major breakdown on the *405!*"

breeders: what homosexuals calls heterosexuals.

buffy: a preppy female. Also, *muffy*.

(to) bump monkies: to have sex. Also, *to boink, to bump, to dip, to rip, to do the nasty, to do the wild thing, to drag the shag, to get busy, to skank, to throw* (him or her) *down, to scrog, to do a session, knockin' da boots, do the bone throw, to poke-a-hontas, to ride the hog, to wax, to wax the knob.*

Buppie: a Black yuppie.

butch: 1.) tough or aggressive lesbian or homosexual. 2.) any tough or aggressive woman.

catcher's mit: a contraceptive diaphragm (also *cum drum, roadblock*).

cave bitch: a White woman.

champ: a male slut. Also, *a yamp.*

cheek speak: phone sex.

cheese kransky: an extremely ugly woman.

chi-chi's: breasts. Also *bazooms, bazooties, bombs, boobs, boobies, cans, cha–chas, hooters, jiggers, jugs, tattas, titties, tooters.*

chicks with dicks: transvestites.

chip trip: a date provided by a computerized service.

chub: a penis. Also, *chubby, chubster.*

(to) clock: to check something out: "That *biddy's* been *clocking* me all night."

clowns: guys — not always pejorative.

cock block: when a guy's friend moves in on his prospective date, preventing him from making further progress.

cock pox: venereal disease. Also, *cock lock, dick sick.*

cock swap: a penile implant.

cooze: a slut.

cradle robber: a person who prefers partners much younger than him or herself.

creep: a weirdo, a nasty jerk. This old standard is popular again, possibly because there are so many of them loose in Los Angeles. Also, *creepo suave, creepo man.*

Dahmer: a highly neurotic freak—a *major creepo suave,* though not necessarily a cannibal.

daisy chain: a group-sex session. Also, *therapy session.*

deeko: a jerk (from *dick* and *geek*). Also, *deeko-seat.*

de facto: one's live-in lover.

dexter: a *poindexter.*

dick: a jerk, male or female. Also, *dickhead* and *dickwad.*

dickless wonder: a wimpy person of either sex. Not to be confused with a *dickless tracy.* (Also see STREETLIFE.)

dingleberry: originally, a little turd that hangs on after a cursory wipe of one's rear end. Now, a jerk.

(to) do: 1.) to have sex with. Adjective, *doable.* 2.) to kill.

doable: sexy (that is, someone you'd like to *do*). Also, *do-able.*

dog: 1.) a man who cheats or treats women badly. 2.) an ugly person, male or female. (Also see EVERYDAY LIFE.)

double bagger: 1.) a person so ugly one needs to put two bags over his head to have sex with him. 2.) a person so promiscuous one needs to wear (or have him wear) two condoms prior to sex (the second meaning has become more common than the first).

double dipper: a bisexual. Also, *bi, switch-hitter.*

doughboy: a fat, out-of-shape guy. (Also see THE SCHMOOZEFEST.)

dork: a nerd, an idiot, a loser. Probably from *dick* and *jerk*. Probable origin of *horkle.*

dry spell: a period of zero sexual activity.

dude: 1.) an attractive but slightly artsy-fartsy male, used by women. 2.) originally a male surfer, but now used for any male. Also, *dudette.*

(to play) dump the chump: a three-person date—so called because the spare boy or girl will eventually be ditched.

818: a person from the valley, a *val.* (From the area code.)

faggot: 1.) a very plain female—that is, one too ugly to be a *real* woman at all (primarily Latino). 2.) a wimp of either sex. 3.) a gay man.

fag hag: a woman who prefers the company of gay men.

farley: 1.) a male homosexual. 2.) an unattractive person.

fatzilla: an overweight person. Also, *munchasaurus*.

fawn: a beautiful young girl.

fellagirly: a lesbian or any woman with both *butch* and *femme* tendencies.

femme: a submissive or stereotypically feminine lesbian or male homosexual.

filth: a *fine* man or any *fine* person: "Girl, he is *filth!*"

filthy: really great looking.

fine: gorgeous. Subsets include *street fine* (naturally gorgeous, without makeup or fancy clothes), *ghetto fine* (inch-long nails, tight clothes, and all), and *model fine* (perfect, but in a made-up, don't-touch-me way). Also, *fine as wine*.

fishing fleet: group of females.

Fleiss chicks: high-class hookers. Also, *Heidi chicks*.

flock: a group of attractive females.

fly girl: a sexy woman. Also, *hottie, finie, cutie*. (Compare to *hood rat*.)

fox: a sexy person. Also, *foxy*.

freak: 1.) an attractive woman. 2.) any person who likes sex—a lot. 3.) an ugly or weird person of either gender.

fresh talent: a prospective date or new lover: "She's not interested in *getting with* you—She's looking for *fresh talent*."

frisky: horny.

fugly: very (fucking) ugly.

full moon: a big rear end.

galimony: support paid by one lesbian to another.

gal pal: 1.) girlfriend, usually platonic, but can also refer to a lover. 2.) euphemistic or libel-ducking term for a woman's lesbian lover.

gas queen: a man who picks up *boulevard boys*.

gaydar: that real or imagined ability to spot a fellow homosexual or lesbian.

get with: to connect socially or sexually: "I'd love to *get with* that *finie!*"

(a) gimme: a promiscuous person, an easy lay. Also, *quicksand, drive-thru, kleenex.* (Also see STREETLIFE.)

good to his mom: homosexual. Also, *flamer* (from flaming faggot), *good with flowers.*

gorgism: exceptional beauty (not to be confused with *lookism*). Superlatives: *full blown gorgism, twitch fire gorgism, major gorgism.*

gaydar

got it going on: (he or she) looks great, is desirable, has a great job, is talented, and so on.

got skills: looks sexy, or, more literally, is good in bed.

granola: noun or adjective meaning hippie, or hippie-like. Also, *crunchy granola dudes, granola dudes, Topangans, Canyonites* (from Topanga Canyon, hot tub capital of the world).

gueen: a transvestite hustler, or drag queen (from *gay boy plus queen*).

gump: a passive homosexual.

hair farmer: person with abundant hair— usually refers to a hardcore rocker.

halfling: a short person.

(to get) hammered: 1.) to be the receptive partner in sex. Also, *to get nailed*. 2.) to get drunk.

gueen

hands off (kind of guy): a sensitive, passive guy; one who never makes the first move.

head to toe: fantastic looking all the way around: "That sweet *finie* is *head to toe*."

helen keller: blind date.

hen party: an all-female party or meeting.

high maintenance: 1.) requiring lots of affection or attention: "Her new gig at Sony pays great, but her boss is *high maintenance*." 2.) requiring frequent beauty treatments: facials, manicures, etc. 3.) a lover who is unreasonably needy.

himbo: a male bimbo.

(to) hit it: to have sex. Also, *to do the spank, to hit the kitten.*

hit one home: to have or cause a *homer,* or orgasm.

ho': 1.) a prostitute. 2.) disrespectful term for any woman.

hog: a *jammy.* (Also see THE WHEEL MEANING OF LIFE.) Also, *chub.*

homeboy/girl: an immediate friend. Also, *homie, homey, homes, homeslice, money.*

homey clown: 1.) imposter or wannabe. 2.) dork.

honey: a cutie, male or female.

honey dripper: an attractive woman.

hoodie: 1.) a pal, a person from the *hood.* 2.) *hood rat.*

hood rat: 1.) a promiscuous girl or woman from the *hood.* Also, *zootie.* 2.) any ratty-looking girl.

(to) hook in: to kiss.

horkle: an idiot, a jerk. Also, *dumbasskiss, dumbshit, dork, dufus, dweeb, dickhead, needs another neuron* (because it takes two to synapse), *RTI* (room temperature IQ).

hot ticket: 1.) a sought-after invitation. 2.) an attractive person of either gender. Also, *hot item, hot number.*

hottie: an attractive female (or sometimes male), a *fly girl.*

hymenally challenged: virginal.

in the club: 1.) pregnant. 2.) gay.

inch boy: a man who has, or is suspected to have, a *teeny weenie*. Also, *bug fucker*.

interior decorating: the sex act.

Irving: a dull-witted person, a bore.

(to) jack off: 1.) to masturbate. 2.) to string someone along. 3.) a jerk. Also, *jerk off*.

jammy: penis. Also *dick, dong, jimmy, john, johnson, john tomas, junior, peter, prick, randy*.

(to) jeep: to have sex in the backseat of a Jeep or any car.

(to) jettison cargo: to get a divorce or to end any romantic or sexual relationship. Also (to give or to get) *walking papers*.

jimmy: *jammy*.

jimmy hat: condom. Also *balloon, coat, cock sock, dubs, doady wrap, raincoat, sock, sweater, glove:* "I told you last time we went out—no *glove*, no love."

jocker: an aggressive homosexual.

joey: a kept boy.

joto: a male homosexual. Also, *puto* (both from Spanish).

joy boy: a young male homosexual.

keeper: 1.) a cherished person, a loved one: "Good looks, good job, good sense of humor—definitely a *keeper*." 2.) any person or thing of value.

(to) kick the ballistics: to smooth talk a prospective date.

Kleenex: a promiscuous person (because you pick it up, blow it, throw it away).

lavender: gay.

lice and fleas: a person suspected of carrying STDs: "Stay away from him, he's *big time lice and fleas*."

load: an overweight person. Also, *got a load on*.

lowball: an unattractive person, a loser. (Also see THE WHEEL MEANING OF LIFE.)

mack daddy: 1.) a cool guy, or one who thinks he is. 2.) a pimp. Also, *daddy mack, mack*.

(to) mack: to make out, to kiss, or have sex. (Also see EVERYDAY LIFE and THE BODY BEAUTIFUL.)

macking tackle: lips. Also, *kissing tackle, French tackle*.

mad bitches: attractive girls traveling in a pack.

main squeeze: a lover or steady partner. Also, *squeeze*. Also, *numero uno*.

mash: heavy petting. Also, *kissfest, kissing party, lumber, mack out, snog*.

meat market: a singles bar, pickup joint.

merkin: an artificial female sex organ.

minky: *pootenany*. Also, *mink*.

miss thing: 1.) a *nellie*. 2.) a cool girl, a girl who's the *bomb*. Also, *Mr. Thang* for a boy.

moe: a male homosexual.

mofo: a term thought by some to be a more acceptable pronounciation of *motherfucker*.

Monet: a person who looks great from a distance (only). Also, a *Seurat*.

mole: a penis (for *muscle of love*). Also, *bozack*, *jimbrowski*.

moneymaker: a rear end.

mosquito bites: particularly small breasts.

mudflaps: a person's rear end. Also *backyard, cakes*.

muff merchant: 1.) a man who picks up female hookers. 2.) a pimp.

nasty: 1.) sexy. 2.) disgusting. 3.) intercourse.

nasty lass: a sexy woman.

nellie: an effeminate gay man, often used affectionately by others. Also, *Sally*.

nimrod: a geek.

no hitter: a virgin.

no-neck: a male jock.

nooky: poontenanny. Also, *to nooky* (to have sex).

o-beast: a person who is overweight and ugly.

oompa loompa: short and stout, from the little people in *Willie Wonka and the Chocolate Factory*. Can be used to describe a person or a body part: *oompa loompa* legs.

open fly: sex-crazed.

O.P.P.: *other people's pussy, penis, property.* Also used as the related verb, to cheat on: "Don't trust him, he's *O.P.P.'n* me."

(not playing on) our team: not of one's sexual orientation, whether gay or straight: "Jack is lovely, but I'm afraid he's not *playing on our team,* dear."

(to) park the love Porsche: to have sex.

(to) pash: to tongue kiss (from *passion*).

(to) pass: to live, or *pass* as heterosexual when one is actually homosexual. From the term once applied to light-skinned Blacks "passing" as White.

peg house: bordello. Also, *crib, jazz joint, rib joint, sin bin, slammer, slaughterhouse, slut hut, snake pit, snake ranch.*

percy bird: a prissy, straightlaced, or nerdy person. Compare to *poindexter.*

(to) perv out: to have kinky sex.

P.I.C.: a close friend (from *partner in crime*). Also, *bosom bud, ace, homeslice, cool breeze.*

pizza face: one with bad acne or scars.

player: a guy who scores a lot, or a frequent dater of either sex. (Also see THE SCHMOOZEFEST, WORK, and STREETLIFE.)

(to) poke squid: to have sex.

poindexter: a geek or nerd—that is, an extremely unhip person, nearly always male. Also, a *dexter*. (Compare to *percy bird*.)

pootenanny: rap slang for female *bootie*—and it rhymes great with *jammy,* too.

poz: HIV positive.

psycho-babe: one who is neurotic but *doable,* if you like to live dangerously. Also, *psycho-chick.*

puddin': vagina. Also, *coozie, kooz, poontang, poon, virginia.*

pugly: very ugly (from *pugly ugly,* or from the Addams Family character Pugsly).

puddin'

puppies: cute boys or girls. (Also see *dogs*/EVERYDAY LIFE.)

quimby: a jerk.

ragamuffin: 1.) a poorly groomed female, usually a young girl. 2.) the Rastafarian version of *rough neck,* i.e., streetwise delinquents.

raspy: ugly, off-putting.

(to be in) relationship turnaround: to be without a partner. (see THE SCHMOOZEFEST.)

ripples for nipples: flat-chested.

rock: a good-looking well-built guy.

rocker: a hard-core rock and roll fan, usually identified by tight clothes and outlandish hair styles.

salt shaker: a person who spreads venereal disease.

saucalicious: sexy (from *saucy*).

scab: an unattractive person.

(to) scam: the ability to sweet talk, especially in romance. Also *to drag, to scoop,* and *kick the ballistics.*

scene: a relationship: "I was into a quickie, but he was looking for a *scene.*"

schwing: 1.) an exclamation meaning, approximately, *that's the most incredibly doable person I've ever seen.* 2.) to have sex or near-sex (with a friendly, as opposed to dirty, connotation).

score: 1.) to successfully make a pickup. 2.) to have sex also, *snag.* 3.) to buy or acquire. (Also see EVERYDAY LIFE.)

screwperstar: a stud. Used primarily in the adult film biz.

sero-discordant: when one partner is HIV positive and the other is not.

session: intercourse. (Also see EVERYDAY LIFE.)

(to) sex: to have sex: "Yeah, my 'rents walked in while we were *sexing*."

shellac head: person who uses too much hair spray or gel.

(to) shoot the gift: to make conversation, especially idle. Also, *shoot the shit*.

to shrimp: to suck the toes for sexual gratification.

side ho: mistress.

skank: an unattractive or unkempt person, usually female. Also, *skag, hag, hagalina, hagster, sea hag, scab*.

skeezer: 1.) a *groupie*. 2.) a *skank*.

shrimp

sketch: a person who is scattered, unfocused, superficial.

(to) slag: to have sex.

(to) slap skins: to have sex.

smooth daddy: a man who is popular with women.

(to) snog: to kiss (originally British).

soap on a rope: a dull or depressed (suicidal) person.

space vixen: a sexy woman: "Everyone was *gassin'* on me last night when I walked into the club with that *space vixen* on my arm."

sketch

(to) spank the monkey: to masturbate. Also, *to beat off, beat the meat, choke the chicken, drop beats, jerk off, punch the dummy, loop the mule, walk the dog.*

(to) spade a chick: to put the moves on a woman.

sploshing: also known as *wet and messy fun,* this is the practice of being covered in chocolate, maple syrup, and other sticky substances for sexual gratification.

spliced: married.

spunk rat: a cute guy.

squallie: a young girl.

square john: a dull man.

squid: a nerd. (See *poke squid.*)

stallion: a virile male—usually said with a snicker.

stank ho': an undesirable woman.

star fucker: 1.) a groupie. 2.) hustlers with attitude (usually *starfucks*).

starter marriage: one's first, which is not expected to last.

steady bone: a pejorative term for a person with whom one is in a relationship just for the sex.

(to) step out: 1.) to date someone other than one's partner. 2.) to have sex with someone other than one's partner: "She doesn't trust me, but I never *step out* on her."

stunts: girls who are, or who one hopes are, promiscuous.

sweetie: a *hottie*.

swettie: an attractive, *doable* female (from *sweaty* and *sweetie* and *betty*.) Also, *sweattie*.

tard: stupid or insensitive person (retarded). Also, *tardo*, and *tardie, tardate, tard off* (for goofy, obnoxious).

tenderoni: a sweet young thing, a girlfriend. Also, *tender*.

thunder thighs: big-legged, overweight.

tig bitties: large breasts.

tire kicker: a frequent dater with commitment *issues*.

tomato (or hot tomato): forties revival slang for a hot chick.

tool: penis. Also, *love tool, chorizo, cobra, hog, pito, pud, manroot, shaft, sinbad, unit*.

trailer trash: poor, uneducated, and ill-behaved White people, whether they actually live in trailers or not. Note that people of other races can live in trailers, but only White people can be *trailer trash*. Also, *trailer folk, trailer people*.

tranzie: transsexual.

(to) trick off: to perform fellatio.

troll: 1.) an aging gay man. 2.) a homeless person. 3.) to cruise, to be on the prowl.

12-play: an extremely enthusiastic, overextended sex act.

two-bagger: see *double bagger*.

(to get) vacuumed: to get divorced (because one often gets *cleaned out*).

valve job: sex in a car. Also, *to coat the interior, to test the shocks.*

virginia: *pootenanny*—that is, a woman's private parts. Also, *box, cavern, folds, drooler, tongue blanket, tunnel, vertical smile, tang.*

walker: a man, often gay, who serves as an escort or date to a woman who is often older, wealthier, or better connected socially, and married to a man who can't or won't attend social functions with her.

wammie: an attractive young woman with purported theatrical aspirations, a *MAW*.

wang: clever person, particularly with computers or electronics (from the computer firm).

(to) wax: to have sex. Also, *to dip the wick* (male only), *to get busy, to do reps, rabbit reps, to do the horizontal boogie, lateral lambada, to do the deed, to get busy, to bump uglies, to rock.*

whistle bait: an attractive person. Also, *date bait, hoot bait, pinch bait.*

wigger: 1.) a person prone to outbursts of temper, that is, a person who *wigs out*. 2.) a White, Asian, or Latin person who is suspected of trying to act and dress like an African-American.

wilma: an unintelligent girl. Sometimes implies unattractive.

winnie bago: an obese person, usually male.

woman years: like dog years, these are calculated differently than a man's: "He thinks thirty-four is too young to get married, but what's that in *woman years*?"

wussy: person who is timid, nervous, lacking courage—a contraction of *wimp* and *pussy*. Also, *to wuss out.*

yahoo: a geek or fool.

yokel: 1.) a *yahoo*. 2.) a local person, a resident of a small or unsophisticated place (from *local yokel*). Usually disparaging.

zootie: a streetwise girl, a little rough around the edges (Latino).

be • bad version • bambino • bando • blow up • **boffo** • book • bootie record • box office • call sheet • cattle call • a cha cha • chantoosie • ciao • **chopsocky** • churban • cock rock • craft • craft service • cut to the chase • deal me evelopment hell • DOA • drop • doughboy • films • flack) flashing • go-see • goebbles • got ears • green room • gr or rewrite • **helmer** • hickey • **high concept** • high schm hit the streets • Hollywood • Hollywood heartbeat • horse bl hyphenate • in the can • indie • indier than thou • Industry ackets • jam • **japananimation** • juice • logline • (to le AW • meatpuppet • ntbslt • offish • Oscar • Oscar nod • er • Pasadena • peeled • pen • pitch • player • playola • press whore • **product** • punch it up • Q • roll calls • sam hmooze • shamefest • show • Sillywood • skeezer • soun tar baggage • starrer • stretch • suit • talking head • tight t • (to throw a) Rudin • toast • **track** • trackers • trades • und • **vanilla extract** • vanity show • wank trade • wet wheel • white label • with a bullet • with an anchor • **wrap** • rty • against the law • Amazon • Ann O'Rexia • b-boys • bad **Baldwin** • Barney • betty • beard • beast • **beer goggl** e-yotch • bell hop • bender • **biddy** • biff • bim • bitch • gnet • bod squad • boxmaster • bomber • bootie call • B eakdown • breeders • buffy • buppie • **cave bitch** • char eese kransky • chip trip • clock • clowns • cock block • c radle robber • creep • dahmer • deeko • **dexter** • dick • s wonder • dingleberry • doable • dog • double bagger • dc / • dork • dude • **dump the chump** • de facto • faggot • g • **farley** • fatzilla • filth • filthy • fine • fishing fleet • cks • flock • fly girl • fox • freak • fugly • **full moon** • ga • gal pal • **gaydar** • gettin' any? • good to his mom • gor iot it going on • got skills • **granola** • halfing • hands off • coe • helen keller • hen party • high maintenance • himbo • ho /girl • homey clown • honey • **honey dripper** • hoodie • h : • hook in • **horkle** • hot ticket • hottie • in the club • l ttison cargo • keeper • kick the ballistics • kleenex • lavenc and fleas • load • lowball • **mack daddy** • mack • mac kle • mad bitches • main squeeze • meat market • miss thi net • mosquito bites • mudflaps • nasty • nasty lass • **nelr** rod • no-neck • **o-beast** • O.P.P. • our team • pash • pa cy bird • P.I.C. • pizza face • player • poindexter • poz • -babe • pugly • puppies • **quimby** • ragamuffin • raspy • cker • saucalicious • scab • scam • scene • **schwing** • sco ot the gift • skank • skeezer • sketch • smooth daddy • sno **p on a rope** • space vixen • spade a chick • spliced • spun quallie • square john • **squid** • stallion • star fucker • steady k ep out • stunts • sweetie • tard • tasty • **tenderoni** • t thighs • tire kicker • **tomato** • trailer trash • tranzie • tr -bagger • umpa loompa • vacuumed • wang • walker • wh • wigger • wilma • **winnie bago** • woman years • wus loo • yorkel • zootie • advertiser • beater • bed dancer • bee ke dyke • bird dog • blew-it • boney • **booted** • braille • b ket • broadie • **bust a left** • buy-n-die • caddie • California ancer • candied • cashmere • cherry • croakwagor tchrocket • cruiser • dorags • detail • din

THE WHEEL MEANING
OF LIFE

Part I: Car Culture and Roach Motels

advertiser: the cheap car advertised in the paper that everybody comes into the dealership *thinking* they want to buy. The salesman's job is to move them, or *stuff* them, into a higher-priced model.

beater: a junky old car. Also, *bucket, clunker, hooptie.*

bed dancer: a minitruck with hydraulic lifts attached to the main frame.

beemer: BMW car (not used for a BMW motorcycle).

bike dyke: street term for a female motorcycle cop.

bird dog: to refer customers to a car salesperson in return for a *spiff.*

blew-it: Buick.

boney: motorcycle. (Also see *hog.*)

(to get) booted: to have an LAPD parking device attached to your car wheel, so that it can not be moved.

(to drive by) braille: to ride on the raised dots in the center of the road in order to stay awake.

brain bucket: a motorcycle helmet.

broadie: the maneuver by which one throws the car into a controlled skid.

(to) bust a left: to make a left turn. Also, *bust a right* for a right turn. Also, *hang a left* or *hang a right*.

(to get) booted

buy-n-die: a Hyundai.

brain bucket

caddie: Cadillac. Also see *hog*.

California car: one that has never left the state, so presumably has not been exposed to bad weather.

cancer: autobody rust.

candied: having a great paint job. Also, *cherried*.

cashmere: a nasty coat of dog or cat fur on the backseat of a car—specifically, one that is to be cleaned prior to sale.

cherry: 1.) adjective meaning *in mint condition*. 2.) a car or bike in such condition. Also, *candied*.

croakwagon: a Volkswagen.

crotchrocket: a powerful, high-performance motorcycle. Also, (for tiny bikes) *pocketrockets*.

cruiser: a car you drive, as opposed to a *showcar*, which is never driven.

derogs: derogatory marks on a credit report. Also used in real estate and other businesses that deal in loans.

detail: to clean a car meticulously, inside and out. (Also see EVERYDAY LIFE.)

ding: 1.) a tiny dent in the body of a car. 2.) a *derog*.

(to) dust 'em: to take off fast, to leave them in the dust.

facelift: the practice of turning back an odometer: "This car's no *cherry*—she must've had a *facelift*."

(to) flip a bitch: *to hang a U-ey.*

(to) floor it: to take off fast, to give it gas. Also *punch it, step on it, put the pedal to the metal.*

Found On Road Dead: Ford. Also, *Fix Or Repair Daily.*

fresh ride: a particularly beautiful car or truck: "You're sportin' a *fresh ride, homes.*"

(to) get your swerve on: to go for a ride.

greenpea: a novice car salesperson, or any novice.

g-ride: 1.) a car stolen for gang activities. 2.) an exceptionally *detailed lowrider.* 3.) A conviction for grand-theft auto.

(to) grind: to whine, tease, torture, or do whatever is necessary to get one's way—usually, to get a desirable price. Past tense, *grinded*: "He really *grinded* me on the *advertiser,* but I did sell him the underbody coat." (Also see EVERYDAY LIFE.)

hog: 1.) a Cadillac or any huge car (also, *land yacht*). 2.) a Harley-Davidson motorcycle or any big bike.

Honda-Bago: an overaccessorized touring motorcycle.

hooptie: a *clunker.* Also, a *bucket.*

hot roller: a stolen car.

(to) ice: to *detail* a car. Also see STREETLIFE and EVERYDAY LIFE.)

jammy: an exceptionally nice or large car or motorcycle. (Also see THE MEET MARKET.)

junker: a beat-up car.

(to) key: to scratch a car's paint with a key.

kojak: *TV parking*: "How do you do it, *girlfriend?* You always nail a *kojak,* and I'm circling the block for hours."

lay-down: An easy sale. Also called a *bend-over. Lay-downs* and *bend-overs* are much coveted by salespeople because they *roll right over.*

lifted: having hydraulics. Also, *slammed.*

limo lock: gridlock at a celeb-heavy event.

lowball: to quote an unrealistically low price over the phone or in an ad in order to get a potential client into the dealership (Also see MORE SLAMS AND PROPS and THE MEET MARKET.)

lowrider: a rebuilt vintage car, customized with elaborate cosmetic work, small wheels, and a specialized suspension that allows the body to be jacked (lifted and raised). The name refers to the visual effect of the car being exceptionally close to the ground.

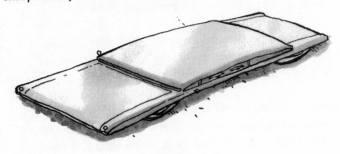

lowrider

Merc: Mercedes-Benz. Also, *Benzo, Panzer.*

98: Originally an *Olds 98,* now refers to any classic car.

passion boat: big, luxurious car, usually something a pimp would drive. Also, *pimpmobile, land yacht.*

(to) pick the cherry: to run a red light.

pleather: (See THE BODY BEAUTIFUL.)

plushed out: having a completely redone interior.

porch: Porsche. (Incidentally, the vogue for pronouncing Porsche with a faux-Germanic final *e,* so that it comes out Poor-shuh, is about over.)

puke-show: Peugeot.

pull-toy: a minitruck. Also, *push cart.*

repo: a car that has been repossessed because the buyer defaulted on payments. Also, *repo man,* for the guy who actually sneaks into your driveway and takes the car.

ride: 1.) any car or other transportation. Also, *wheels, transpo.* 2.) the person giving you a ride: "Michelle, your *ride's* here and he's a *hottie!"*

ro-ro: a roll-on, roll-off truck used, instead of a tow truck, to move an incapacitated vehicle: "My car's worth eighty grand—send that tow truck back to the shop and send me a *ro-ro!"*

roach: a would-be car buyer with bad credit.

roach coach: a mobile kitchen.

roach motel: 1.) a car dealership specializing in extending credit to *roaches*. 2.) a *roach coach*.

road pizza: a dead animal by the side of the road. Also, *road hash, road kill*. (Also see STREETLIFE.)

roscoe: a right turn.

shaggin' wagon: a luxurious car (one with a big backseat for *shaggin'*). Also, *passion boat*.

shotgun: the passenger seat. Also, *to ride shotgun*.

six-fo': the ultimate *lowrider*, a '64 Impala.

smeg: 1.) disgusting nickname for auto leather wax that will be understood by anyone who ever took boys' hygiene in high school. 2.) *to smeg* a car seat.

spiff: 1.) the payment, or finder's fee, made to a *bird dog*. 2.) any tip or gratuity. Also, *to spiff*.

(to) squeeze the lemon: to hurry up to make a yellow light. Also, *punch the sun*.

(to) stuff: to convince someone to buy something he didn't know he wanted: "We don't have a red on black Acura—stuff 'em into the mauve *tone on tone*."

surface streets: any street or road that is not a freeway. Also, *to go surface*: "The *10* would have been faster, but he's phobic, so we had to go *surface*."

tone on tone: a car that's the same color inside and out.

toolin': driving around. (Also see EVERYDAY LIFE.)

Toyopet: a Toyota, from the original name used in the United States. Also, *toy*.

transpo: a vehicle of any sort (*transportation*).

trokita: a minitruck.

trunkie: car wash or car lot customer who has half of his possessions stuffed in the trunk of his car. Also, *trunker*.

TV parking: parking that's too good to be true—that is, close, immediate, and legal (from the unrealistic ease with which cars are parked on television).

U-ey: a U-turn. Also, a *louie, to flip a bitch*.

(to be) upside down: to owe more on a car (or anything else) than it's worth.

Waldo: a CHiPs officer.

wheels: *transpo*.

yeah-you-are: Jaguar (from the faux-British pronunciation affected by some owners: *jag-you-ah*).

yard trophy: a disabled car.

yell bell: a car alarm.

zonin': taking a ride in the car.

Part II: Destinations: From the Motherland to Smurf Village

Avenues of Design: what the West Hollywood PR reps wish you'd call the area south of Santa Monica Boulevard where a number of interior designers and upholsterers have set up shop.

(the) Bev Cen: the Beverly Center shopping center.

BH: Beverly Hills.

BK lounge: Burger King.

(the) Blue Whale: what the West Hollywood *flacks* wish you wouldn't call Pacific Design Center, an enormous jewel-blue monolith on Melrose Avenue. See *Green Giant*.

(the) Boo: Malibu. Also, the *'Bu.* (Also see THE MEET MARKET.)

borscht belt: the Fairfax district (from the heavily Jewish, elderly population).

Boys' Town: West Hollywood (from the large gay population). Also, WeHo.

bronzeville: East Los Angeles (from the largely Latino population).

Central Avenue: synecdoche for the legendary hotbed of jazz, long gone.

charcoal alley: a famous shopping complex in Watts.

cotton curtain: a mythical dividing line between White areas and Black.

(the) County Museum: Los Angeles has a lot of county museums, but the only one so called is the Los Angeles County Museum of Art, often gauchely referred to by its acronym, *LACMA*.

Eastside: the eastside of the city of Los Angeles consisting of mostly lower-income families, immigrants, and *real* artists.

flats: the flat streets of Beverly Hills below Sunset Boulevard, as opposed to the often—but not always—pricier hilly areas to the north.

(the) 5. (See the *ten*.)

(the) 405. (See the *ten*.)

ghost town: downtown Los Angeles.

golden triangle: the financial districts of downtown L.A., Century City, and Orange County.

(the) Green Giant: the other half of *the Blue Whale*.

(the) hills: the Hollywood Hills.

Hollyweird: Hollywood (used for both the place and the concept). (Also see THE SCHMOOZEFEST.)

Insane Diego: San Diego.

Jack in the Crack: Jack in the Box Restaurant.

kili cali: Southern California.

L.A.: a written and spoken abbreviation sometimes frowned upon by the natives, but much preferred to *El Lay* and the despised *La La Land* and *Lotus Land*.

Los Angeles, City of: Is it a place? Is it a frame of mind? Geographically, oddly enough, the city of Los Angeles encompasses several neighborhoods in the San Fernando Valley, including Sherman Oaks and Studio City. See *valley*.

Lotus Land: see *L.A.*

Mexican Rodeo Drive: Broadway, downtown (for its many shops and vendors). Also, *little Brazil*.

Mickey D's: McDonald's. Also, *Mac's, Mick D's*.

MLK: Martin Luther King Boulevard, a main thoroughfare through South Central Los Angeles.

MOCA: the Museum of Contemporary Art. Also, *TC,* for the Temporary Contemporary.

morebucks: Starbucks (the pricey coffeehouse chain).

(the) motherland: South Central Los Angeles.

mouschwitz: Disneyland (used by employees).

(the) nickel: skid row (downtown).

NoHo: North Hollywood.

no-man's-land: the eastern area of downtown, where the artists' lofts are.

(behind the) Orange curtain: Orange County, the county to the south of Los Angeles, consisting mostly of wealthy suburbs. Often used disparagingly by terminally hip Angelenos.

over the hill: 1.) *Valley* parlance for the city of Los Angeles, or specifically, Beverly Hills. 2.) *Hollywood* parlance for Burbank (where many TV studios are located).

(the) Palisades: Pacific Palisades. Also, *Pali.*

PDC: Pacific Design Center, properly, though seldom, written without the article *the.* Also, *the Blue Whale.*

Pedro: San Pedro, L.A.'s main port.

People's Republic of Santa Monica: a sobriquet earned by Santa Monica's strict rent control laws and tolerance for street people. Also, *SaMo*.

(the) Pink Palace: The Beverly Hills Hotel, which is actually painted Pepto-Bismol pink and mint green. Not to be confused with the *Palace*, a venerable nightclub.

ring toss: a nude beach.

Saliva Lake: Silverlake.

smurf village: any White middle-class suburb.

(the) southland: television newspeak for the greater Los Angeles metropolitan area that has, horribly, moved into common parlance.

So Paz: South Pasadena.

swish alps: Silverlake (for its large gay community).

Tar-Zhay: faux French pronunciation of the name of the deep discount store, Target.

the ten: the 10 freeway. For no obvious reason, some freeways are known by name, some by number. For instance, *the ten* is actually the Santa Monica Freeway, except where it's the San Bernardino Freeway, and the *405* is the San Diego Freeway. That's going south. North of LA the *405* becomes the Golden State Freeway but is usually known as the *5*. The Hollywood Freeway is the segment of the 101 that runs north to south, although the off-ramps mark its direction east and west. Where the 101 actually runs east to west, it becomes the 134, which goes to Pasadena and is called the Ventura Freeway, not to be confused with the Pasadena Freeway, or 110, which is called the Harbor Freeway if you're heading south, unless—oh, never mind.

valley: often disparaging term for the San Fernando Valley and the towns therein. See *Los Angeles*. Also, *valley girl, val speak, vals*. The synonym *818* can be used as a noun or as an adjective: "She's from Santa Monica but her *stilo* is totally *818*."

WeHo: West Hollywood.

Westside: Los Angeles, west of Robertson Boulevard, including Santa Monica, West L.A., and Beverly Hills. The Westside is a place, a demographic, and a state of mind.

EVERYDAY LIFE

Anklebiters to Yadda Yadda Yadda

-able: suffix that makes a noun or verb an adjective: *doable* (sexy), *bagable* (not worth keeping), *crankable tunes* (those worth playing loudly—originally surferese).

action: 1.) a noun used to intensify any other noun to which it is attached: "Major traffic *action* on Wilshire Boulevard." 2.) sex or romance: "Think I'll see some *action* tonight?"

-age: a suffix that turns any word into surferese: *herbage* (for herb, or pot), *tunage* (for music), *scarfage* (for food).

agenda: ulterior motives: "He didn't buy those $500-a-plate charity tickets from sheer goodness. He's got an *agenda*."

all: see *like*.

(to) attend class: to watch television.

ATM: a generous, wealthy man, especially one's father (from automatic teller machine): "Her mom's a waitress, but her dad's an *ATM*." Also, *wallet, wallet carrier, money machine.*

(to be) all over (something): to be very excited. "Do I want to go? Damn, I'm *all over* that!"

alcoholya later: good-bye (a play on *I'll call you later*).

(to) attend class

ampin': excited. Also, *amped* and *amped up*.

Angeleno: annoying but necessary appellation for a resident of the city. What else are we going to call them? *Los Angeleans*?

anklebiter: a *rug rat*. Also, *no-neck monster*.

. . . as he has to be: very. Usually used with a compliment, as in *"fine as he has to be."*

as if: no way! (an expression of disbelief).

at the end of the day: when all is said and done. Also, *bottom line.*

attitude: a haughty or belligerent attitude: "She's got serious *attitude*, and not much to back it up." Also, *attitudenal*. See *'tude.*

(to be) audi: to leave (homonym for *out of here*.) Also, *Audi 5000, chowdie, to bail, to bounce, to book, to ditch, to jam, to motor.*

back: bodyguard or moral support (from *backup*): "I'm going in, and you be my *back*." (Also see THE MEET MARKET.)

backslider: 1.) person who reneges, who goes back on his word. 2.) person who breaks his own resolutions, as to quit smoking or quit drinking.

baggage: unresolved personality problems. Also, *emotional baggage* and *pack your bags, we're going on a guilt trip.*

(to) bag some z's: to sleep. Also, *to clock z's, to catch z's.*

bag that: forget that. (Compare to *to bag on*/MORE SLAMS AND PROPS.)

(to) bail: to leave. Also, *to bill.*

(to) ball hog: *to bogart.*

(to go) balls out: to pursue victory with vigor and aggression. "If you want that account, go *balls out.*" Also, *all out balls out.* Similar to *balls to the wall.*

barhopper: person who hangs out at bars. Also, *to barhop, to clubhop, clubbie, clubber, juice hound, night crawler, player, scenester.*

bash: a party.

bass-ackwards: mixed-up, *ass-backwards.*

basshead: person who blasts music from a *boom box,* especially heavy bass dance music—a play on *basehead* (a freebase addict).

beam me up, Scotty: tired expression meaning time for a *reality check* (from *Star Trek*). (Also see *beam up*/STREETLIFE.)

beaucoup: just like the French word for very, but pronounced boo-coo: "*beaucoup bucks.*"

beef: 1.) a problem or complaint. 2.) to have a fight or an argument: "So I stayed out till three A.M.! You got a *beef*?" 3.) to fall or hurt yourself: "I was *bookin'* on my new *blades* 'till I *beefed*."

been-there-done-that: an expression of world-weary *ennui*.

belig: belligerent.

beveg: an alcoholic beverage.

BFD: acronym for *big fucking deal*. Also, *SFW* (for *so fucking what*).

big time: very, certainly, or majorly: "He's *big time loaded*."

bigs: cigarettes. Also, *bones, cancer sticks, grits, sticks, coffin nails, lucys.*

bitch: 1.) tough or unpleasant situation, as in "ain't that a *bitch*," or "*payback's* a *bitch*." 2.) an inanimate object, such as a car or airplane, used admiringly: "that Viper's a *bitch*." (Also see THE MEET MARKET.)

bitch slap: a literal or figurative slap across the face, often said playfully: "He's late again, I'm gonna *bitch slap* him when he rolls in."

Black tax: 1.) the mythical—but much credited—tax charged to African-Americans on everything from insurance to real estate. 2.) the higher cost of many goods—such as groceries—in the ghetto.

blah-blah: boring or expendable details: "Yeah, so you got stuck in traffic, spare me the *blah-blah*." See *yadda yadda yadda*.

(to) blend: to mingle: "I've never been to this club—let's *blend* awhile and check it out."

(to) blow: 1.) to suck, to be lousy: "This party *blows*."
Also, *blows the big one, bites the big one.* 2.) to leave.
Also, *to blow da spot* (to leave immediately). 3.) to perform
fellatio. 4.) to smoke 5.) cocaine.

(to) blow a gasket: a tired expression meaning to
become irate.

blowing up my spot: blowing my cover.

(to) bogart: to hog everything, to be selfish, originally
with a joint, now with anything: "Hey, man, don't *bogart*
the chips, they're for everybody."

(to) bomb over: to visit, to go: "Let's *bomb over* to John's
new crib."

(to) book: 1.) to hurry. 2.) to leave.

boom!: a verbal exclamation point: "We walked in, he saw
Donna, and *boom!* that was it."

boom box: a large portable stereo or car stereo.

bonus: an exclamation of delight: "You've got *wheels*
tonight? *Bonus!*" (See also THE BODY BEAUTIFUL.)

(to) bosh: to end something, to kill it (from *kibosh*). Also,
to *put the bosh on* something.

bounce: to leave the room. Often used as a threat: "Yo, I
told you I don't like your face, so *bounce!*"

boy: cherished friend: "Frank's my *boy*, I love the guy."

bra: bro, or brother—a friendly appellation, sometimes
used for females.

brain fart: a clumsy error, a careless remark.

brain surgery: any difficult task, usually used in the negative: "Why can't you balance the checkbook? It's not *brain surgery*." Also, *rocket science, rocket scientist, Einstein*.

(to) break bad: to act in a menacing fashion: "He cut me off, I *flipped him off*, he tried to *break bad*, and I made *tracks*."

break (someone) off some: 1.) to give something, usually lip: "*Don't* take that shit, *break him off some*." 2.) to kill or beat someone.

(to) break on: to tell off or to insult.

(to) breathe blue: to stay calm. New Age *mush-speak*, from the reputed color of a calm aura.

bro-duding: conspicuous male bonding: "Matt and Pete are *bro-duding* over a couple of brewskis and the Clippers game."

broham: friend, amigo, loved one. Also, *brochick*, for a female pal or tomboy.

bud: 1.) friend. 2.) marijuana.

buggin': overly excited, angry, frustrated: "Why you *buggin'* on me like that, *homes*? Just *chill*."

buggyman: a homeless person (from *shopping buggy* and *bogeyman*).

bummed: depressed, down in the dumps. Also, *dumpster city*.

(to) bump sounds: to play music. Also, *to bump*.

bum rush: to push into a place that is sold out, closed to the public, or to which one has not been invited: "So we're not on the *list*—let's *bum rush* the door!"

burly: exceptionally cold: "It's *burly* out tonight."

(to) bust a move: to make a move, to take some action: "I know she's gonna *shoot me down,* but she's so fine, I gotta *bust a move*." (Also see THE WHEEL MEANING OF LIFE.)

busted: 1.) caught in the act. 2.) broke, bankrupt.

buttload: what, in gentler days, was called a *boatload*— that is, a whole lot.

buzz: 1.) scuttlebut, hot gossip. 2.) phone call: "Give me a *buzz* this afternoon." 3.) visit, drop in: "*Buzz* by this afternoon if you can." 4.) a very short haircut, a crewcut. 5.) the state of being high: "Man, I got a *buzz* off the fumes from that bus."

(to handle one's) buzz: 1.) to remain calm and cool. 2.) to appear sober when intoxicated: "Sue drank too much, but she can *handle her buzz*."

caj: 1.) casual: "Dress *caj* for the cruise." 2.) no problem: "Don't worry, that's *caj*."

California Roll: 1.) a roll of sod with grass already on it, named for its similarity in appearance to the nouveau sushi. 2.) the practice of driving up to, but not stopping for, a stop sign.

cel: a cellular phone. Also, *horn* (for any phone).

cel hell: where you're left if the person you're talking to puts you on hold (because *cel* calls are so expensive).

(to get or to be) centered: to be calm and focused.

-central: a suffix denoting a place (literal or figurative) where the aforementioned thing is found: *bim central, action central,* hard times *central.*" (Also see *-fest.*)

century: one-hundred-dollar bill, a *c-note.* (Also see *yard, year.*)

changes: originally the pains of withdrawal from heroin, now used to describe any problems or difficulties: "I had to go through *changes,* but I got you the tickets."

chargin': ready to go, eager, anxious: "He was *chargin'* to hit the waves." (Also see *charger*/THE BODY BEAUTIFUL.)

check please: a phrase used to end a conversation: "Did you say my girlfriend just walked in? *Check, please!*"

check this: check this out, listen to this.

check yourself: a warning, meaning think about what you're doing/saying. Also, *run a check.*

chi-ching!: overly expensive.

chicksdiggit: why men pretend to like or be interested in things they're not, really. "Why is he going to the Everything But The Girl concert? *One word: chicksdiggit!*"

ching-kwon dough: a person with a lot of money.

chill: 1.) calm down, be cool. 2.) hang out, relax. Also, *chill out, cold chillin', chillin' like a master villian, chillin' like Bob Dylan, kickin' it, loungin', crazy loungin'.*

chilly: a beer. Also, a *cold one.*

(to) chunder: to vomit. Also, *to blow chunks.*

classhopper: a student who repeatedly skips classes.

clean: well groomed and well dressed. (Also see STREETLIFE.)

clica: a group of friends, clique.

clickin': going crazy, pissed off: "I tried to talk to him, but he was *all* clickin'."

clit lit: feminist literature, or the study of same.

(to) clock: to look at, to check out. (Also see STREETLIFE and THE MEET MARKET.)

to close (someone's) book: to tell him off. Also see *read*.

(to be) cold maxin' out on the ill tip: to sit back and relax.

(to make a) collect call: to get someone else to pay for something: "Let's go to Eric's and *make a collect call*—I'm starving!"

color it dos: make that drink a double, or make it two drinks (from *dos*, Spanish for *two*).

color me-: prefix that emphasizes the adjective to follow: *color me* embarrassed, *color me knocked out, color me* pissed.

(to) come off: 1.) to appear: "He *comes off* like a *poser*." 2.) see *go off*.

(to) come real: to be upfront about opinions, feelings: "I love you, but if you don't feel the same, just *come real* with me."

(to be) comped: to be treated, to have the tab picked up (originally Vegas slang). (See WORK.)

confuser: what many over thirty call a computer.

cooked: 1.) drunk or stoned. Also, *baked, fried, lit, zapped, wasted, sapped*. 2.) in trouble, similar to "His goose is cooked."

cool breeze: pal, friend (used as a greeting: *"S' up, cool breeze?"*). Also, *money.*

(to) cop: 1.) to obtain by any means, especially by theft. 2.) to confess (short for *to cop a plea*). 3.) to have, to adopt, as in "He *copped* an *attitude.*"

(to) cop a squat: 1.) to pull up a chair. 2.) to go to the bathroom.

CRS disease: that's the one where you *Can't Remember Shit.*

(to) crank it up: to turn it up, increase the volume or magnitude: *"Crank up* those *sounds, girlfriend!"*

(to) crash: Originally, to come down from a drug high. Now, to go to bed or go to sleep. Also, to *catch z's.*

crazy: very: "That sound is *crazy dope.*" Also, *mad.*

crew: originally, a street gang or graffiti-painting gang. Now, any group of friends. Also, *posse.*

crib: home.

crusties: 1.) old hippies. 2.) any senior citizens.

cut to the chase: skip the BS and get to the point.

cyberpunk: a literary style that borrows heavily from sci-fi, *roman noir,* and biology.

cyclist: psychiatrist (short for *trick cyclist*).

dead presidents: folding money, bills. Also, *presidents, prezzies.*

(to) deep six: to kill a plan, to forget about something. Literally, to bury something six feet under, as in a grave: "She tried to *break bad* with me, but I told her to *deep six* that shit."

default paradigm: what happens if no other plan is enacted: "If my check doesn't arrive in time, we're a few days late on the rent. That's the *default paradigm*."

(to get) detailed: to get well groomed and dressed. To *get clean*. (Also see *detail*/THE WHEEL MEANING OF LIFE.)

deuce: two dollars. (Also see STREETLIFE.)

dime: a five-dollar bill. (Also see STREETLIFE.)

(to) dine and dash: to duck out of a restaurant without paying. Also, to *D and D*, to *play dine and dash*, to *chew and screw*.

dinero: money (Spanish). Also, *moolah*.

DINK: Describes a childless couple (Double Income, No Kids).

disco nap: Disco is long gone, but a quick nap before all-night partying is still very much alive.

(to) dish: to gossip.

doctor feelgood: a physician known to prescribe recreational drugs. Also, a *croaker*.

do me solid: do me a favor. Also, *do me a solid*.

dogs: 1.) any items or objects, nearly always used in the plural: "Load them *dogs* on the truck and we're outta here." Also, *doggies, pups, puppies*. Compare to *big dogs*. 2.) close friends: "Don't mess with those guys, they're *my dogs*." (Also see THE MEET MARKET.)

dome burner: 1.) a perplexing situation or problem. 2.) high-grade marijuana.

done: see *cooked*.

done deal: an agreement, or a sure thing.

don't even trip on me: don't get upset. Your boss comes over with an evil look on his face. You say *"don't even trip on me."*

don't go there: that's a subject better left unmentioned. Also, *don't play that, don't take me there.*

don't sweat my technique: 1.) don't copy me, you'd never get it right. 2.) don't criticize me.

double o: extremely aggressive or outrageous behavior. (from *G double O double F*, see *go off*): "Check the way *home boy* drives! He's *double o!*"

double o's: Kool cigarettes.

down: 1.) *phat.* 2.) prepared, willing: "Dinner? I'm *down.*" 3.) proficient: "Man, when it comes to handling money, he's *down* with the *big dogs.*"

drama: a hysterical outburst or scene: "Oh, God, I missed my deadline by two hours. Now the editor's gonna bring on the *drama.*"

(to) drop a dime: to make a phone call, or more specifically, to rat on someone.

(to) drop science: to teach a lesson, to instruct, to set someone straight: "Those ignorant fools, I'm gonna be *dropping science* on 'em in no time." Also, *to school.*

(to) drop the digits: same as *to drop a dime.*

ducats: 1.) money. Also, *ducks, duckettes, dukats, duckies, bucks, buckeroos, bones, cash, dinero, dough, 'fetti* (from *confetti*), *green, lean green, mean green, loochie, paper, government art collection.* 2.) tickets.

duh: that's obvious, that's a given. Often, *well, duh.*

(to) duke: 1.) to fight. Also to *throw chingasas.* 2.) to tip: "*duke* the waiter so we can *book.*"

E-ticket ride: an exciting trip or experience. From the now-defunct system at Disneyland, under which the most exciting rides required an *E-ticket.* Also, *E-ride.*

earth to ___: used with a person's name, implies that he is out of touch with reality. See *beam me up, Scotty.*

elvis: gone, out of here: "Hey, I'd like to help, but I'm *elvis.*"

ends: money (from *dividends*).

E.N.D.: Escape 'N' Denial. Used to describe somebody who will not admit to his or her obvious problems: "We go shopping and she tries to fit into a size four when she should be in a *twelve!* She's totally *E.N.D.!*"

(to) fade: to ignore, to snub. (Also see THE BODY BEAUTIFUL.)

fat bank: lots of money: "That car, those *threads*—that cat's got *fat bank.*"

fat grrrls: a feminist movement that encourages women to take pride in being large (from *riot grrrls*).

fat pockets: rich.

fen-phen: affectionate moniker for the diet drugs fenfluramine hydrochloride and phentermine resin.

-fest: a suffix meaning "a gathering of," or "a party to celebrate" as in a *weaselfest,* a *blamefest,* a *babefest.* Note that a *bitchfest* might be either a party full of women, a party full of gay men, or a meeting at which everyone is complaining.

fin: a five-dollar bill. Also, *finski, five-spot, fiver.*

(to be) finnin' (to): to be getting ready to: "I'm *finnin' to* go to the party about eleven." Also, *fittin' to* (from *fixing to,* an imported Southernism).

flack: static, backtalk. (Also see WORK.)

flavor:
1.) style, flair.
2.) the tone or mood of a situation: "Wait here, I'll run inside and check the *flavor.*"

(to) flex: to display expertise. (Also see STREETLIFE.)

(to) flip (someone) off: the age-old gesture of giving the finger. Also, to *give someone the bird.*

(to) flip (someone) off

(to) float (one's) boat: to pique one's interest, usually used in the negative: "I like *sounds* but classical music just doesn't *float my boat.*" Also, *water my tree, spark my motor, raise my flag, gun my motor.*

(to) flounder: to blow it: "I *floundered* that test."

(to) fold: to give in, to fail to *stand up*.

folk: ordinary people, nice people. (Compare to *folks*/THE WHEEL MEANING OF LIFE.)

(to) follow (one's) bliss: *mush-speak* for doing whatever you want to do.

foodie: a person who knows a lot, or thinks he or she knows a lot, about food.

for sure: surely. Often used sarcastically, to mean the opposite.

forties fever: midlife crisis.

(the) 411: information. "What's the *411* on that new kid?"

(to) free it up: to release certain information, to tell all.

full on: 1.) completely, fully: "He is *full-on babelicious.*" Also, *full-blown.* (Also see *gorgism*/THE MEET MARKET.) 2.) "Yes, I'm in complete agreement."

fully: the preferred way of responding in the affirmative. Also, *damn straight, right on, straight up, totally, that's affirmative, that's a go.*

game over (or game): that's it or that's enough.

(to) gas: to be excited and/or full of enthusiasm for something: "We saw Tarantino's new flick last night—I was *gassin' on it!*"

get out: I can't believe it! Also, *get out of town, get out of here.*

G.F.I.: acronym for *go for it,* give it a try. Also, *take a shot.*

giddeup: the beginning: "He was no good from the *giddeup*." Also, *get-go, git-go, day one, jump street.*

girlfriend: just what it sounds like, used as a friendly appellation for a friend or stranger (originally hip-hop, now universal).

glitter and sneeze: salt and pepper.

(to) go: to say: "So I *go*, how was the party, and he *goes*, I thought you'd be there—"

(to) go off: 1.) to be exceptionally exciting: "That party's going *to go off*." (Also, *come off*.) 2.) to perform exceptionally well: "Check out Raggs on his skateboard, he's *goin' off*!" 3.) to *go ballistic*: "I was ten minutes late and he just *went off* on me."

(to) go postal: to become insane with rage. Also, *to go mental, to go richter*.

(to) go south: to end, to be ruined, to be destroyed: "I asked him to catch a *flick*, but that plan *went south* when his *squeeze* showed." Also, *to get deep-sixed*.

good on ya': see you later, have a good day, 'bye for now.

goths: scary-looking fans of gothic rock music who wear dead-white makeup and black eyeliner with dyed-black hair.

grill: face: "Wipe that sneer off your *grill*."

(to) grind: 1.) to eat. 2.) to wheedle, to hard-sell. (Also see THE WHEEL MEANING OF LIFE.) 3.) to slow dance with hips close. 4.) to have sex.

grip: a bunch, a lot: a *grip* of *smokes*.

(to) grizzle: to sleep. Also, *to catch z's*.

(to) groove: to enjoy, to kick back. (Also see *groovy*/ MORE SLAMS AND PROPS.)

(to get your) groove on: to dance: "Hey, sister, *get your groove on*."

grub: 1.) baby: "Gotta run, time to feed my *grub*." 2.) food.

(to) grub: to eat: "We were *grubbin'* down." Also, *to mow, to scarf*.

grunts: food.

hack: 1.) a game of Hacky Sack. 2.) a third-rate professional.

hair ball: very challenging and scary: "No way, *dude*! That ski slope is *hair ball*!"

half-caf: coffee that's half decaf, half regular. Also, *no fun* (non-fat), *speed ball* (straight espresso), *unleaded* (decaf).

(to) hang: 1.) to fraternize, *to hang out*. 2.) to bond, to become close. 3.) to endure, *to hang in there*: "Yeah, our relationship's a little rocky right now, but I can *hang*."

(what's the) haps: what's happening, what's going on?

(to have a) hard-on: to be very enthusiastic: "Jane's got a *hard-on* for that new CD-ROM." Not to be confused with *being* a *hard-on*, which is to say a jerk, pig, or an autocrat.

harsh: 1.) difficult, unpleasant. 2.) to speak harshly: "Stop *harshing* on me."

(to) harsh a gig: to expose, to blow a cover: "I *stepped out* on Tom, and his sister *harshed my gig*."

(to) harsh a mellow: to disrupt an otherwise calm mood or situation. Also, to *freak my buzz, freak my nerves, work my nerves, get a freak on.*

hasta: good-bye (literally *until*, from the Spanish phrase *hasta la vista*, popularized to the point of exhaustion by *The Terminator*).

(to be) hating life: to be frustrated and depressed.

(to) haze: to *harsh:* "I tried to be cool, but he was *hazin'* me the whole time."

headbanger: 1.) a therapist, a shrink. 2.) a fan of heavy metal music.

(to have) a heat on: to be drunk: "You'd better drive, I think Mary's *got a heat on.*" Not to be confused with having a *hard-on*, which is also possible for Mary.

hel-lo: 1.) that's obvious. 2.) snap out of it, wake up and smell the coffee: "*Hel-lo*, that was a red light you just sailed through."

hey: 1.) all-purpose greeting, what used to be *hi*. 2.) all-purpose exclamation that can mean anything from "yes, I totally agree with you," to "I don't know about that, bro." Also, *say hey*.

hi-didge: expensive (from *high digits*).

hipster: a person in the know, e.g. a *fashion hipster*.

(to) hit: to go to, to visit: "Let's have a drink at Red, then we'll *hit* Le Colonial for dinner." Also a single toke off a cigarette. Not to be confused with *hit it*, which is to leave: "Ready to *hit it*? Let's *bail.*"

hondo: a tourist.

'hood: short for neighborhood—can be used literally or figuratively: "I don't know what city Leon grew up in, but you know he's from the *'hood.*"

(to) hoof it: to walk.

honeywagon: any ladies' room—originally the trailer used as a women's bathroom on a film set.

(big ol') honkin': used as a modifier to emphasize size or magnitude: "a *big ol' honkin'* cold sore," a "*big ol' honkin'* earthquake."

(to be) hooked up: to be *dialed in*, well connected. Also, *to be hooked in*.

(to) hook up: 1.) to meet, to get together. 2.) to provide whatever is necessary: "Just sit down at the table, I'll *hook you up* with some dinner." Often, simply *to hook*.

(to) hoover: to consume lustily: "She *hoovered* that Fatburger."

(to) hose: to trick or tease: "Seriously? You *hosin'* me?" Not to be confused with *being* a *hose*, or a loser.

hot flash: a bit of news, often used sarcastically: "Here's a *hot flash* for you—our date was *last* night!" (shortening of *hot news flash*).

howsy-bra?: how's it going, brother?

(to) hurl: literally or figuratively, to vomit. Also, *to barf, blow, blow chunks, earl, hug the bowl, lose your guts, puke, drive the porcelain bus, talk to the big white phone, technicolor yawn*.

I don't THINK so: no way, no chance, that's ridiculous.

ice: 1.) very cool: "those *kicks* are *ice*." 2.) to give the cold shoulder: "I tried to hit on her, but she *iced* me." (Also see THE WHEEL MEANING OF LIFE and STREETLIFE.)

intervention: a confrontation in which a person's (self-proclaimed) friends and loved ones present him with a list of social crimes before hauling him off to *rehab*: "Lisa's in heavy denial about her addiction, so we're planning an *intervention*. You bring the corn chips."

in the wrapper: in bed.

issues: unresolved psychological problems, *baggage*.

jacks: dollars.

jack shit: zero, nothing. Also, *jack, squat, diddley squat*.

jam: 1.) a party. 2.) a musical number. 3.) to work hard and fast 4.) to succeed. 5.) to leave rapidly. 6.) to party.

jammy: a penis.

jive: bullshit, nonsense (the noun, adjective, and verb forms of this old favorite are back—or still—in style).

joe six-pack: an average guy.

jones: both noun and verb forms were originally used to describe a heroin addiction. Now used for any strong need or desire: "Frank's *jonesin'* for that *biddy* at the bar," or "That *biddy* at the bar's *got a jones* for Frank." Also, *fiendin'*.

kegger: a type of party where beer is served on tap (from a keg).

keyed: excited, anxious. A newer form of *keyed-up*.

kick: trend, hobby, avocation: "He's on that jazz *kick*." (Also see THE BODY BEAUTIFUL.) Also, *tip*.

kick back: 1.) relax. (Also see *kickin' it*.) 2.) wait a minute, don't jump the gun. 3.) easygoing: "Don't worry, he's way *kickback*."

kickin': great, happening: "The Lava Lounge was *kickin'* last night."

kickin' it: relaxing.

(to) kick it to the curb: to put an end to something: "She doesn't go out *clubbing*—she *kicked all that to the curb* years ago." Also, *to the curb* for lousy, not very good.

kinkoid: 1.) person who works at Kinko's copy shop. 2.) person who frequents Kinko's. 3.) an afficionado of kinky sex.

lacto-ovo: a *lacto-ovo* vegetarian—that is, one who eats milk and eggs.

(to) lamp: 1.) to sit back and relax: "Somebody check Mike—is he *lampin'* or is he dead?" Also, *whilin'*. 2.) to hang on the street corner.

last call: for alcohol (closing time).

lates: good-bye (short for *later*, which is short for *see you later* or *catch you later*). Also, *late, later on*.

latronic: surferese for *later on* (said when leaving).

(to be) like: to think, say, feel, or do: "So I'm *like*, this is really uncomfortable, and she's *like* all *twisted up* over it." Also *all, all like*: "She's *all* this is my fault, and I'm *all like* trying to say it's not." (Usage of *like*, along with *all* and *go*, is so pervasive that few people are, *like*, aware that they say it . . . and nearly everyone does.)

Lincoln drop: In a store, the dish of pennies by the cash register to which one can add or subtract as appropriate. Also, a *need one—take one*.

(on the) list: that is, on the clipboarded list of names that tells a nightclub bouncer who is to be a) treated royally, b) treated well, or c) allowed in at all. Pretty girls are typically "on the list" whether their names appear there or not. Also see *UD*.

loaded for bear: 1.) angry (as in a shotgun that's loaded with sufficient ammunition to kill a bear). 2.) intoxicated.

loofa: a person who comes to visit you from another country and ends up staying longer than anticipated. In other words, a foreign sponge.

lookism: what used to be called the tyranny of beauty. Granting or expecting favorable treatment on the basis of looks. Also, *looksism*.

(to) lose (something): to get rid of: "Wanna *lose* that smirk, pal?"

low tide: a state of depression: "Pass me some chocolate, will you? I'm *low tide*."

lurch: an undertaker.

mack out: 1.) to eat vigorously: "We *macked out* at Denny's at three in the morning." 2.) passionate kissing. Also, *mack down*. 3.) to dress well or to over dress.

mad: abundantly, extremely: "This scene is *mad* noisy — let's *book*."

mad quantities: lots and lots.

major: very. Also, *majorly*: "I'm *majorly* into that *dude*."

mall rat: a person, usually a young girl, whose favorite sport is shopping, and whose favorite meal is french fries with diet coke.

master: a suffix that, added to a noun, means "master of that thing or activity": *spliff-master* (knowledgable about marijuana), *tube-master* (excellent surfer). Also, *meister*.

meltdown: the condition caused by stress overload.

mindfuck: 1.) disturbing or highly perplexing: "That new Boredoms record is a *serious mindfuck*." 2.) extremely impressive 3.) to mess with someone, to tease or trick.

money: an affectionate greeting used by men, for men. Also, *cuz, cool breeze, homeslice, bro, brother, bra, G., bunchy, killer*.

moolah: money.

(to) morph: to change to a bizarre degree: "I used to like Nikki, but since she got a promotion she's *morphed* into some kind of post-human specimen."

(to) motivate: to be motivated, or to get moving: "You didn't wash these dishes yet? Well, haul your ass downstairs and *motivate*."

multi-culti: multicultural.

murky: depressed.

mush-speak: icky language used by New Age and self-help afficionados. Also, *psychobabble, touchy-feely, crunchy granola*.

my bad: my fault: "Whoops, I think you're right—*my bad!*"

my shorty: my pal, my confidant.

nectar: the best, the most beautiful. "Check out my wife's sister, she's *nectar.*"

nectar of the gods: beer.

newby: a newcomer, a novice (originally computerese).

N.F.C. party: one where *no fat chicks* are allowed.

(my) niggas: my close friends, my pals (used by and about all races).

nine deuce: the year 1992. Also, *nine trey, nine fo', nine fi', nine six,* and so on. No word yet on how to handle the millennium.

nip factor: the outside temperature, or an inquiry as to how cold it is: "What's the *nip factor*?"

nippy: cool (thermally), an old-fashioned word that's back in style.

no-brainer: 1.) obvious. 2.) simple, easy to do. 3.) stupid.

no diggity: no kidding, usually used sarcastically. He says, "Whoops, I *bummed* all your *smokes.*" You say, "*no diggity.*"

(to give a) nod: 1.) to endorse (see *Oscar nod*). 2.) to acknowledge: "Even if we don't use Raymond's tracks on our album, we ought *to give him a nod* in the credits."
3.) when written *NOD,* a *notice of default,* as on a car or real estate loan. (Also see *derogs*/THE WHEEL MEANING OF LIFE.)

no doubt: I agree. Also, *I hear you, I heard that, I'm picking up what you're throwing down, we're on the same page.*

noir: Originally *film noir,* a style defined by its bleak cynicism and crime themes—now used to describe anything with an edge.

not!: just kidding, or I don't agree (overused and now considered *lame*).

not even: see *as if.*

(to) nuke: 1.) to microwave, as a breakfast burrito. 2.) to kill, as an idea or plan. 3.) to get extremely intoxicated or high.

odious maximus: describes something that stinks, literally or figuratively.

oil spill: a visit from a rich relative who pays for everything: "Just when the landlord was putting my gear out on the street—saved by an *oil spill!*"

on the flipside: tomorrow: "Catch ya on the *flipside, homeslice.*"

on point: right on the money.

one word: a simple explanation, though it can be more than one word long: "What do I think of the military look? *One word,* it *blows.*"

(to) open the lunchbox: to pass gas.

orange men: the men who sell bags of fruit and peanuts by the side of the street. Also, *fruit ambush.* (Although lots of women do this, too, no one ever says *orange women,* or *orange people.*)

(to be) out: 1.) to be gone, especially a person: "Later, I'm *out*." Also, *out of here* (see Audi). 2.) to be openly gay, *out of the closet*. 3.) to be out of fashion: "Those flair jeans are *out*."

(to) out (someone): to expose his or her homosexuality or any other secret: "Tiffany said she's in training for the marathon, but we *outed* her at *Mick-D's*."

owner: what you become when there's no turning back: "Cancel the wedding? Honey, I'm pregnant. You're an *owner*."

(to) own: to have mastered something: "She *owns* the slopes."

p's: parents.

(to) pack a lunch: to leave town: "Another mudslide? Let's *pack a lunch*." Also, *pack it in, pack it up*.

pad: home, house.

paging Jack Meoff: an expression of contempt (from the proverbial trick played on hotel bellhops, at least in adolescent fantasy).

parkma: parking karma, or the ability to find good space easily.

payback: revenge. Often, *payback's a bitch, ain't it?*, meaning, *serves you right*.

payed-ass fool: a person with a lot of money.

peace out. good-bye. Often, just *peace*. Or, just *out*. Also, I'm *scissors* (for I'm *cutting out*.)

peep da flava: roughly, *watch this, my friend, and see how it's done.*

peep it out: the nineties way to say *check it out.*

peeps: 1.) people, especially one's staff or representatives: "Have your *peeps* give my *girl* a *buzz* and we'll *take lunch*." 2.) sunglasses.

petro: worried (from *petrified*).

pissing match: argument: "I asked that clerk for change for a *fin,* and he wanted to get into a *pissing match* about it."

pity party: just what it sounds like, but you hold it for yourself. That's the one you hold for yourself when you're feeling *Murky:* just you and a couple of six-packs (or a pint of Chocolate Ripple, depending on your inclination).

plastic: 1.) credit card. 2.) phony.

(to) play someone: (Also see WORK.)

plexin': stressed, uptight.

(to) pose: *to front,* to fake it.

(to) preach: to tell the truth, to instruct, to speak up. Often used to urge a speaker on: "That's right, Leon, you tell him. *Preach!*"

premeditated murder spree: PMS (premenstrual syndrome). Also, *hell-bent for chocolate.*

prendida: overly excited (from Spanish).

(to) process: to consider and understand something completely: "Yes, I heard you say you're in love with your *trainer,* but I need time *to process*."

psych! Just kidding. Also, *psych out, psyched you out.* (Compare to *psyched*.)

psyched: psychologically prepared, excited, ready to play or ready to win. (Compare to *psych!*)

pull it over: admonition to come down to earth, make a *reality check:* "Tell that guy to *pull it over,* will you? He's way off base!"

(to) pull the plug: 1.) to put the *bosh* on a project or idea. 2.) to commit suicide.

(to) pump: 1.) to turn up the volume: "Pump those sounds!" 2.) to question thoroughly, to debrief: " I already *pumped* her about the new boss."

(to be) pumped: to be excited. Also, *pumped up.*

punch: what you do now that phones don't have dials: "*Punch* in Judy, will you, and see if she's *down* for lunch."

(to) radio that: shut up: "You can *radio that shit,* or we can *dance.*"

rag: to nag and complain. Also, *rag on* and *rag out.*

(to) rage: to enjoy oneself, with a connotation of wild activity: "That party went *richter* last night, man—*out of control.* Everybody was *raging!*" Also, *to get down, party down, party hard, go richter.*

ramboid: excessively excited.

read: 1.) to tell someone off: "I read *him, Miss Thing,* and then I *closed his book.*" 2.) to see right through someone or something.

(to make a) reality check: to think things over, to be sure you're being realistic.

redux: a popular diet drug, similar to *fen-phen*.

'rents: parents. Also, *parental units, units* (from *Saturday Night Live* — old but still in use).

(to) represent: to be true to your beliefs, culture, people.

retail action: shopping. (See *action*.)

'rettes and chez: cigarettes and matches. Also, *smokes and fire*.

(to) riff: to insult or boast.

rift: *flack*: "I'm getting *rift* about my purple hair."

road rage: why that pleasant-looking matron in the Chevy Blazer just gave you the finger.

(to) Rodney King 'em: to administer a merciless beating, whether literal or figurative: "Butch, *roll* into that meeting and *Rodney King* 'em!"

ROF, LOL: an adjective meaning funny. From computer shorthand for *rolling on floor, laughing out loud*.

(to) roll: 1.) to hang, to be with your friends: "I'm *rollin'* with my *crew* today — I'll be back around four." 2.) to overwhelm or attack: "We're going to *roll* on his *crew*." 3.) to drive.

(to) roll in: to arrive.

(to) roll out: to get going, or to leave.

romp: a silly adventure, a lark.

rooted: devastated: "He never called back and Jennifer's *rooted*."

roried: broke, without funds.

rug rat: a small child. Also, *dwarf, grub, little, spawn*.

run a check: shut up, think about what you're saying, or take a self-inventory. Also, *check yourself*.

run a make on that plate: a warning or admonition to check something out, to be sure of what you're saying.

run tape: the equivalent of *I've heard this before*: "So you had to work late, *yadda, yadda, yadda—run tape*."

Santa Ana: a strong seasonal windstorm believed to originate in the Santa Ana mountains. Also, *devil winds*.

(to) scam: 1.) to maneuver, to hustle. 2.) to pick up or try to pick up someone of the opposite sex.

scarfing material: food. Also, *scarfage*.

(to) score: 1.) to achieve or accomplish a goal. 2) to steal. (Also see THE MEET MARKET.)

screenager: what teens are called in the nineties.

(to) screw the pooch: to slack off, to waste time (originally British).

(to) scroll (something) by: to repeat, from computerese: "*Scroll* that plan *by* me again, will you, *bud?*"

session: any activity done with great gusto—conversation, drug taking, often sex.

(to) set up: to accommodate, to take care of.

shade: a suntan: "Let's go *kick it* at Zuma and get some *shade*."

shit: this word has more meanings than *aloha* and, like *stuff*, can be used to mean virtually anything. You can *be* the *shit*, *have* the *shit*, *talk* the *shit*, *know* the *shit*, or just *look* like *shit*. But it is most often used to mean "the ultimate": "That new album is the *shit!*" Also, the *bomb*, the *butters*.

shocker: a bad day.

shoegazer music: slow, often boring music. Also, *elevator music* for muzak. Also, *yawn-core*.

(to) shoot down: to reject, as in a plan or a person.

shout: one's turn to pay for a round of drinks: "Hold your *wad*, this is my *shout*."

(to) shut: to finish or to ignore: "He knew Tom called a meeting, but he *shut* it."

sighting: sighting of a celebrity: "We'll take your *'rents* by the Four Seasons for a *sighting*, then we'll *hit* the shops on Rodeo Drive."

sketchy: 1.) iffy, unlikely. 2.) lacking detail (as a *sketchy* plan).

slaudian frip: a Freudian slip.

smack: street slang: "His *smack* is so thick he needs subtitles."

(to) snake: 1.) to sneak: "We had a pass to the premier, but we had *to snake* to avoid the line." 2.) to steal.

social X rays: very thin, rich women of a certain age — that is, over twenty-eight (coined by Tom Wolfe, now in general usage).

S.O.L.: acronym for *shit out of luck:* "Sorry, *last call* was at two o'clock. You're just *S.O.L.*"

sounds: music. Also, *tunes, tunage, toons, vibes, grooves, jams, jammies, tracks.*

(to) spank the plank: to play guitar.

(to) spark: to light (as a cigarette).

speedbump: 1.) a boring person. 2.) any obstacle, literal or figurative. 3.) a homeless person. 4.) what real surfers call body surfers.

(to be) spent: to be exhausted. Also, *shagged, beat, whipped, wiped out*, and *flat out like a lizard drinking* (Australian).

Spring Street: a synecdoche for the *Los Angeles Times* newspaper.

square: a pack of cigarettes. Also, *woodchuck* for a pack of cigarettes or for any tobacco.

square bidness: honest, full of integrity: "Murray won't rip you off, he's *square bidness.*"

squirrely: *sketchy*, out of control (similar to its standard, but uncommonly used, definition).

stack: 1.) exclamation meaning *super, right on.* 2.) money: "Don't mess with my *stack.*"

star sixty-nine: how one pronounces *69, a phone service that allows a subscriber to dial back his last unanswered call: "Don't worry if I don't pick up, I'll just *star 69* ya."

static: difficulty, trouble. Also, *flack* and *backflack*.

(to) step up: to help someone out. *Stand-up* guys used to *do the right thing*. Now they *step up* (from *step up to the plate*).

stick: billiards: "Let's shoot some *stick*." (Also see *stick/* THE BODY BEAUTIFUL.)

stop it: see *get out*.

(to be) strapped: to be broke or short of cash. Also, *busted*. (Also see STREETLIFE.)

stressin': upset, uptight: "I told her I'll be on time, but she's still *stressin'*." Also, *stressin' it, stressin' out, stressed, stressed out, plexin', tweakin'*.

stupid: very. Usually modifies a *prop* as opposed to a *slam*: "That CD is *stupid fresh*." Also spelled *stoopid*.

(to get) styled: to be treated well, to be comped: "I got *styled* at the club—the doorman let me in free and *set me up* for drinks."

s'up: short for *what's up*. Used as a general greeting. (*What's up* is still used to mean *what's happening, what's going on*: "He knows the score, he knows *what's up*.")

(to) suss out: to find out, to snoop around.

(to) swirl: to show off, present, or promote: "He's been *swirlin'* his new screenplay all over town."

(to) tag the lawn: to urinate in public. Also, *to write* (one's) *name, to water the plants*.

take: interpretation or approach: "What's your *take* on the police scandal?"

talk to the hand: Somebody gets right up in your face. You show 'em your palm and say "talk to the hand." Can be challenging or placating.

(to) talk trash: 1.) to talk nonsense. 2.) to insult. Also, *trash talking, playing the dozens.*

tapped out: 1.) broke, without money. 2.) empty, used up: "I don't have any fresh ideas for the ad campaign, I'm *tapped out.*" Also, *assed out, tapioca.*

textbook: well executed, done perfectly: "Did you see how he picked up on that *biddy*—it was *textbook.*" Also, *classic.*

thank you for sharing: oh, shut up.

the: article often preferred, in surferese, when standard usage would call for *a* or *an*: "That's *the killer ride, homes.*"

third wave: 1.) nineties feminism, considered less militant than that of the seventies' *second wave.* 2.) the third stage of any political movement or art form.

(to go) thrifting: to go shopping at thrift stores.

(to) throw a mental: to throw a fit.

(to) throw a seven: to die. Also, *to buy the farm, to cash in.*

(to) throw (someone) under the bus: to betray or refuse to help someone, or to make him the scapegoat: "I coulda took the rap, but I *threw him under the bus.*"

tight: drunk or high on drugs. (Also see THE SCHMOOZEFEST and MORE SLAMS AND PROPS.)

ticker: the heart—literal or figurative.

tip: a thing that is heavily influenced by another: "That rapper is heavy on the jazz *tip.*"

tizwoz: angry or flustered (originally British).

toast: *history*: "One step closer, and you're *toast*." Also, *out the door*, and *out*.

to' down: drunk, *wasted* (from torn down). Also, *to' up*.

tool: 1.) a verb meaning to steal or to mess with: "I left the *yell bell* off and I got *tooled!*". (Also see THE WHEEL MEANING OF LIFE.) 2.) penis.

totally: 1.) completely (used for emphasis). 2.) yes, I agree with you. (Also see *fully*.)

track: a recorded song, a *cut* off a record.

tree hugger: an environmental activist. Also, *bunny hugger*.

tribe: group of peers, or clique: "Yeah, I like Lola's, but the people who hang there aren't my *tribe*."

(to) trick: 1.) to spend money. 2.) to soup up (usually, to trick out): "He *tricked out* his sixty-five Eldo with low-profile rims." 3.) to have sex. 4.) to have sex for money.

trustafarian: wealthy White kid who dresses in hip-hop or reggae style clothes and spends his or her time surfing or skiing (a play on Rastafarian).

trust fund baby: wealthy kid who spends his or her time partying, whether or not he or she actually has a trust fund.

'tude: *attitude*. Can be complimentary or the opposite, often denotes pretentious posturing.

(to) turn (something) out: this is one of those odd phrases with several related meanings: to push something over the edge, to make it happen, to introduce someone to a new activity: one can *turn a party out* (heat the party up) or *turn it out* while partying (get personally heated up, or drunk) or one can *get turned out* at a party (that is, lose his virginity). To *turn someone out* can also mean to introduce him to his first gay act or his first act of prostitution.

(what's your) twenty?: crossed-over CB talk for *where are you*?

24-7: all the time (twenty-four hours, seven days a week).

UD: undesirables. Shorthand for the list of people banned from a club or restaurant: the *UD* list.

under the ether: in the happy daze induced by a really good salesperson's successful pitch: "I didn't need three new Prada bags, but I went *under the ether*."

upspeak: the style of speech in which every statement sounds like a question. You know?

UVs: sunshine. Also, *rays*.

(to) vege: to do nothing, literally or figuratively: "His parents want him to go to college, but he'd rather just *vege*" (from *vegetable,* and *vegetate*).

vegan: a true vegetarian, one who eschews all animal foods, including milk, eggs, and honey and usually, animal products like leather, wool, and silk. Pronounced vee-guhn.

veggie: 1.) vegetable. 2.) "vegetarian" of any kind, including one who eats chicken and fish. Also, *bush doctor, bushman.* See *lacto-ovo.*

vibe: 1.) ambiance, mood of a place or situation. 2.) to give off *bad vibrations:* "I walked in there, and right off the guy starts *vibing* me."

video moment: a cherished moment (similar to a Kodak moment).

voice jail: where you go when you're hopelessly lost in voice mail menus.

wad: 1.) money. 2.) orgasm (to shoot your *wad*).

(to) walk the walk: to try to play the part, try to fit in (from *walk the walk and talk the talk*).

way: very: "way cool."

weight: problems, troubles. (Also see STREETLIFE.)

whasup widdat?: an expression of confusion.

whatever: an expression of disgust, boredom, or of reluctant compliance.

what's your stilo?: what's your flavor, what's your scene, what are you all about?

(to be) whipped: 1.) to be beaten. 2.) to be exhausted. 3.) to be ruled by one's female partner (from *pussywhipped*). (Also see STREETLIFE.)

white bread: 1.) boring, ordinary, bland. 2.) a White person who is considered to be the preceding.

whole nine: everything, all the way (from *the whole nine yards*).

(to be) wiggin': to be overagitated.

(to) windbag: to talk excessively about insignificant subjects: "That class was a *snooze*—she was *wind-bagging* from the *giddeup*."

(to) windbag

word: I agree, that's right. Also, *word up*.

(to) work: 1.) to use something to its maximum potential, or to excel at something. One can *work that bootie, work that thing*, or just *work it*. 2.) to take advantage of someone: "She thought he was into her, but he was just *working* her for her contacts." 3.) to hassle, to berate, possibly to the point of violence. More often, *to work over*: "When she found out he was just *working* her, she really *worked him over*."

yadda yadda yadda: so on and so forth, or "You know the rest without me explaining." Also, *run tape; spladdy-dee, spladdy-dah; dot-dot-dot*.

yard: 1.) one-hundred-dollar bill: "A quick bite at Drai's'll set you back about a *yard*." Also, *yardski*. 2.) one thousand dollars (this older meaning is now seldom used).

year: a one-hundred-dollar bill. Also, *a Franklin*.

MORE SLAMS AND PROPS

A-list: first choice, the best. From parties, casting lists, etc., that have an *A-list* of first-round invitees or choices, and *B-* and *C-lists* to draw on as the *A-list* regrets.

abfab: great *(absolutely fabulous)*.

aggro: intense, done with gusto and pizzazz.

all balled up in (one's) underwear: confused.

all that: an adjective meaning terrific or fabulous: "You just think you're all that, don't you?" (from *all that and more*).

all the way live: exciting, outrageous: "Your party was *all the way live!*" Also, *big time, way live*.

(must be) amateur night: the West Coast version of *bridge and tunnel* people, that is, what you blame when the lines are too long at a movie or concert.

aujourd'hui: French for *today,* used to mean "very hip" in place of *au courant:* "That's *so aujourd'hui.*"

awesome: fabulous.

babe: a cutie, male or female. Often, a *total babe*.

babelicious: gorgeous, sexy, *doable*.

bad: yes, they're saying it again, and it means what you think. Also, *baddest*.

bad people: singular (not plural) form, meaning a liar, thief, or backstabber—especially one within one's own social circle. (Compare to *good people*.)

(to) bag on: to criticize. (Compare to *bag that*/EVERYDAY LIFE.)

(the) beans: great, the real stuff.

big dogs: heavyweights or VIPs—what used to be called *big boys* or *fat cats*. Also, *pissing with the big dogs*.

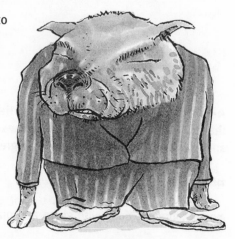

big dogs

Big Kahuna: a VIP, or someone who thinks he's one (very dated surferese, originally Hawaiian). Also, *big cheese, cheese, cheesola, wheel*.

big ups: gratitude, respect. Also, *props*.

bionic: awesome, large, or with great vigor. (Also see THE BODY BEAUTIFUL.)

bitchin': great, cool (originally surferese, now dated).

bodacious: large, impressive (originally Southern, from *bold and audacious*).

(the) bomb: the best: "That new cut's *the bomb*." Also, *the butters*.

bonus: an exclamation meaning *great!* (Also see THE BODY BEAUTIFUL.)

brutal: adjective or exclamation meaning anything from mildly unpleasant to unbearable: "The nanny was sick and I had to watch the kids all day by myself—*brutal!*"

buck wild: crazy, complete disorder.

bummer: see *nightmare.*

buster: 1.) a wise-ass. 2.) the African-American version of a *slacker.*

butt rash: something that is extremely irritating. Also, *butt itch, gold bond moment, (gets your) panties in a wad, (gets your) shorts in a knot.*

butt ugly: particularly hideous.

buzz kill: a person, situation or thing that *kills* a literal or figurative buzz. A cup of coffee after a drink is a *buzz kill.* So is your *squeeze* walking into a *babefest* where you're *jammin'.*

cadet: a space cadet, that is, a person who is slow or out of it (old, but still widely used).

cheesy: 1.) chintzy, cheap. 2.) campy, ostentatious Vegas style—used to describe anything from clothing to music.

chiz: the best, the coolest: "It's the *chiz,* babe" (from the Spanglish pronounciation of *shit*—that is, *chit*—and from the ad campaign "It's the cheese.").

clueless: mixed up, confused, or just *out of the loop.* Also, *without a clue.*

cold: 1.) ruthless, cold-blooded. 2.) very, very cool.

cold rollin': bullshitting, jiving, idly boasting.

come off it: stop being pretentious or annoying. Also, *come down off it, come down off that:* "You think your *assistant* needs an assistant? *Come down off that.*"

copacetic: a third generation is now using the word, which still means *everything*'s *okay.*

core: a positive description of something powerful, intense, serious. That is, *hard-core:* "Whoah, *dude,* that John Woo flick is *core!*"

(to) crack on: to *slam:* "Stop *cracking* on my *ride* unless you want to *hoof* it."

crasher: 1.) a (physically or socially) clumsy person. 2.) a party crasher.

cut: 1.) adjective meaning muscular, well built. Also *buff, tight.* 2.) a *slam,* a *crack.* 3.) a recorded song composition.

cutter: a backstabber.

daggy: 1.) *skanky,* slutty looking. 2.) bull daggy.

(to do) damage: 1.) to excel: "Girls, step out on that runway and *do some damage.*" 2.) to cost a lot: "That wrap party at Cava *did some damage* to my *plastic.*"

def: cool, hip (dated).

delish: sweet, wonderful (delicious).

Disney: bright, colorful, and artificial: "Her face is so *Disney* it needs more maintenance than a Studebaker in Alaska."

(to) dog: 1.) to nag or criticize: "Stop *dogging* me!" 2.) to pursue relentlessly (a back-formation, from the adjective *dogged,* meaning determined). (Also see THE MEET MARKET.)

dope: great, cool, awesome (now considered dated).

down: hip, cool, and *dialed in.* Also *knows what time it is.* (Also see EVERYDAY LIFE.)

downright upright: see *righteous.*

edgy: 1.) cutting edge, the latest and newest. 2.) having a dark, or sinister edge.

epic: extremely cool or great.

fab: fabulous. That is, anything from tolerable to breathtaking. Also, *fabuloso.*

flaco: Spanish for *skinny,* often used affectionately.

flavor of the month: 1.) the latest trend. 2.) one in a string of many love interests.

flaw nigga: a poseur.

fly: cool, sexy, desirable (now dated).

FOAD: acronym for *fuck off and die* (pronounced foe-add).

fool: this word, meaning what it always has, has been repopularized by rap and hip-hop slang. Also, *brain donor, horkle.*

forehead: a big idiot. Urban legend says this term was coined by *Ahnold.*

for real: really, it's true. Often used in the interrogative: *for real?*

foul: ugly, unappealing (often used with ass, as a *foul-ass* smell, a *foul-ass 'tude*).

fresh: hip, new, exciting (somewhat dated).

(to) front: to fake it, to *pose:* "That *m.f.* has been *frontin'* the Black Power word, but he's not even registered to vote!"

frosted flake: a pretentious person, a show off. Also, *Tony the Tiger.*

(to) fuck it up: 1.) to do something well and with great style: "*Check* the way he rides—he *fucks it up.*" 2.) *to fuck up*, to bumble.

fuck up: a bumbler, a loser.

gee: a jerk, especially a male, senior citizen jerk. Usually, an *old gee* (pronounced as in geezer): "Watch your left, that *old gee* needs driving lessons." A *gee* is not to be confused with a *g*, and an *old gee* is not to be confused with an *OG*, or *original gangster*. (Also see STREETLIFE.)

golden: special or great—practically untouchable.

good people: singular form for a person who is honest, kind, upright: "You can trust him, he's *good people*."

groggins: really great, *epic.*

groovy: means just what it meant thirty years ago. And you *still* have to be under twenty-one to say it with a straight face.

half-stepper: person who does something halfway, doesn't follow through. Also, *a flake, to flake.*

hard: ruthless, cruel, but often used positively: "Ice Cube's new track is *crazy hard.*"

hellacious: scary or horrible. Also, *hellified, hairy.*

helluva: fabulous, *groggins.*

hideous: unbearable, undesirable, unattractive, or simply ridiculous. Also, *fucked, fucked up, heinous, lame.*

history: gone or finished. "That *look* is *history.*" Also *yesterday, last year, last week's news, tired.*

horror show: exploitative, shocking, wild.

huge: 1.) fabulous. 2.) very famous: "Barry Manilow is *huge* in Australia."

ill: 1.) bad-ass, streetwise, ruthless. 2.) excessive in any context. 3.) incredibly great: "His interpretation of Hamlet is *ill.*" Also, *sick.*

illified: the best, something modified to be the ultimate. Also, *illin'.*

insane: great, exciting.

in the zone: spaced out (for *in the Twilight Zone*). (Also see *zoned.*)

jamoke: a loser, a chump.

jerk off: a jerk, from the phrase's original meaning, to masturbate. *Jack off* shares both meanings.

jurassic: out of date, out of style.

killer: great. Often used as an affirmative, replacing *yes,* or *okay, cool.*

(to be) knocked out: 1.) surprised. 2.) overwhelmed (as *knocked out* by her beauty, *knocked out* by his charm).

lame: out of fashion, old, not fresh, or poor quality. Also, *lame-ass* (as an adjective or noun), *late, old, over, tired, worked.*

large: great, fabulous, indulgent, extravagant. Also, *livin' large.*

loked out: souped up, improved. Describes a car, computer, or anything that can be *tricked out* with extras (from *loco*). Also spelled *loqued out.*

loud: an adjective that has crossed over to adverb form; an adverb meaning excellently, with great vigor: "Navratilova plays tennis *loud.*"

L7: 1.) not hip, square (from the shape the letter and numeral form). 2.) prison or jail.

mad: abundantly, extremely: "This scene is *mad* noisy. Let's *book.*"

mad cow: nutty (from the disease). Also, *crazy cow:* "Stay out of his way, he's gone *mad cow* about the advertising presentation."

mad skills: exceptional talent.

magoo: a pathetic or laughable older man (from the cartoon).

mint: 1.) great, fantastic, gorgeous. 2.) in perfect shape, as in *mint condition*.

moldy: unwell, ugly, out-of-date, or undesirable. An all-purpose *slam*.

monster: 1.) epic, great. 2.) enormous or oversized: *monster tires, monster beats*. (Also see THE SCHMOOZEFEST.)

mulled up: confused.

naff: of inferior quality, boring, dull (originally British).

nectar: beautiful, gorgeous. Also, *neck:* "She's *neck!*"

new school: the latest, most cutting edge thing. (Compare to *old school*.)

nightmare: the nineties update of *bummer*. Describes any unpleasant experience from nuclear holocaust to being served a cold cup of coffee.

nineball: a loser.

no-hoper: a lost cause.

nugget: *epic*.

old school: 1.) classic, original, with a positive connotation: "Damn, those platform shoes are *old school!*" 2.) old-fashioned, out of date: "You're thinking *old-school;* gotta get with the nineties."

on: 1.) praiseworthy, timely, and to the point: "The music *blows,* but your lyrics are *on.*" 2.) self-conscious, conscious of one's effect on others (from *onstage*).

out of control: exciting to the point of being overwhelming: "The Batman ride at Magic Mountain is *out of control.*"

out there: strange, wacky.

phat: *epic.* Sometimes written *fat.*

pimpy: stylish, cool, groovy: "*Dude, pimpy kicks!*"

played out: overused, *worked.*

poser: one who *poses,* that is, a poseur. Said ironically, or not.

prada: exceptional, first-class (from the pricey designer line): "Mike's sister is total *prada.*"

primo: prime, the best (pronounced *preemo*). (Also see STREETLIFE.)

props: kudos, respect. Usually, *to give props.* From proper respect. Also, *propers.*

psychosanitarian: a person obsessed with cleanliness, a neatnik. Also, *OCD* (from *obsessive compulsive disorder*).

psychosanitarian

rad: fabulous, terrific. Also, *radical* (both are dated but still in use).

random: 1.) unfocused, scattered, unpredictable: *"What's up* with John? First he wanted Alicia, then Beth—he's so *random."* Also, *ambig.* 2.) to express the chaotic, illogical nature of an event or situation. "Fireworks, hula dancers, motorcycles, it was so *random,* I loved it."

raw: 1.) a general term of approbation. 2.) sexy.

real deal: honest, *for real.* Also, *real deal homey feel.*

richter: 1.) great, *smokin',* incredible. 2.) upset: "I told her I just wanted to be friends and she went *richter* on me!"

righteous: upright.

Ringo: a novice, a person who lacks experience.

rocket: very cool, great: "That fine babe's a *rocket."* Probably evolved from *to rock:* "That babe's *rockin'."*

(to have the) sauce: to be troublesome and hard to handle—used admiringly: "She's a handful—she's really *got the sauce*."

scary: 1.) crummy, ugly, cheap, tasteless. 2.) awesome: "My ten year old is designing our website—it's *scary*."

(to) shred the hane: to be exceptionally proficient at something. Originally surferese for aggressive surfing.

sick: exceptionally cool, epic.

simple: describes a person who is stupid: "Shut up, *simple*."

(to) sinead: to blow a great situation: "Careful, or you're gonna *sinead* it." (Pronounced *shin-aid*, from the singer, Sinead O'Connor.)

slacker: shiftless *Gen-X* dilettante.

slam: an insult. Also, *to slam, to cut, to crack on, to bag on.*

slammin': great. Not to be confused with a *slam*.

sleazebag: a morally challenged person. Also, *sleazeball, slimeball, slimebag,* and *scumbag.*

smack magnet: a person who picks up and uses the latest slang with ease.

slam

smeg: garbage, scum, anything disgusting. Also, *schmeg*. (Also see THE WHEEL MEANING OF LIFE.)

smokin': *epic, slammin'*.

snaps: 1.) kudos, *props*. Popularized by *In Living Color*'s film-critics routine. 2.) criticisms, *cracks*. 3.) paper money.

snooze: a bore: "His poetry is a *major snooze*."

spaced: out of it. Also, *spacey, spaced out*.

spaz: 1.) a clumsy person. 2.) to fumble, to malfunction.

spun: emotionally unstable, psycho: "That chick is *way spun*."

stand up: righteous, honorable: "Trust him; he's rich, but he's *stand up*."

stoked: happy, excited, enthusiastic.

strokes: similar to *props*, but often given insincerely, by mandate, as to a loathsome superior: "Cathy needs her *strokes* or she won't meet her deadline."

(the) stuff: *upright,* or the best.

stylin': happening, *aujourd'hui*.

sweet: *clean, cherry,* exciting, great: "*Check* that *sweet ride*."

tardate: stupid, ridiculous (from retarded). Also, *tard, tardo, tardish, tardy*.

tasty: fine, of high quality (often, but not always, describes a person).

TB: short for *true blue* — honest, loyal.

ted: a nerd.

thick: 1.) fat. 2.) stupid. 3.) emotionally close: "We go way back, we're *thick*."

tight: 1.) buff, toned. Also *cut*. (Also see THE SCHMOOZEFEST and EVERYDAY LIFE.)

to' up: in bad condition, *trashed* (from torn up).

trashed: 1.) ruined. 2.) drunk. Also, *bombed, ripped, smashed, wasted, lit, twisted.*

trech: cool, ruthless, tough (from *treacherous*) Also, *trechie.*

trendoid: a person who slavishly follows trends.

troll: a homeless person. (Also see THE MEET MARKET.)

trophy wife: any subsequent wife who is younger, more beautiful, more accomplished, or richer, than one's first.

true school: honest, the *real deal, old school*—but perfectly valid today.

(to be) tweaked: 1.) bothered, irritated: "Relax! Why you *tweakin'* so hard?" Also, *torqued.* 2.) stoned.

twisted: 1.) perverted. 2.) worried, upset. 3.) stoned or drunk. 4.) confused.

walk toward the light: New Age admonition to drop dead.

weasel: 1.) a noun meaning *sleazebag.* 2.) a verb describing what *sleazebags* do: "He's *weaseling* on the deal."

whack: 1.) outrageous, crazy, mind-blowing. 2.) terrible: "Your *track* is *whack*."

(to know) what time it is: *to be in the loop, to be down, dialed in.*

wicked: 1.) great. 2.) sexy.

wild: describes an experience anywhere from absolutely incredible to barely noteworthy: "Yeah, we had lunch and went shopping. It was *wild*." (Also see STREETLIFE.)

wild hair: something that irritates.

(to be) wooded: to be excited, enthusiastic, *to have a hard-on*, or a *woody*, for something.

woodsy: cool.

worker bee: an ordinary person, often said disparagingly: "She divorced a *money machine* and now she's seeing a *worker bee*."

yesterday's news: boring, old-fashioned, out of style. Also, *five minutes ago, last week, last year.*

you're the man: 1.) you're the boss: "I got no *beef, you're the man*." Also, *Charles in charge*. 2.) you're cool, you're number one.

zoned (or zoned out): spaced.

be • **bad version** • bambino • bando • blow up • **boffo** •
book • bootie record • box office • call sheet • cattle call
a cha cha • chantoosie • ciao • **chopsocky** • churban •
cock rock • craft • craft service • cut to the chase • deal m
evelopment hell • DOA • drop • doughboy • films • flack
) flashing • go-see • goebbles • got ears • green room • gr
or rewrite • **helmer** • hickey • **high concept** • high **schm**
hit the streets • Hollywood • Hollywood heartbeat • horse b
hyphenate • in the can • indie • indier than thou • Industry
jackets • jam • **japananimation** • juice • logline • (to l
AW • meatpuppet • ntbslt • offish • Oscar • Oscar nod •
er • Pasadena • peeled • pen • pitch • player • playola •
press whore • **product** • punch it up • Q • roll calls • sam
hmooze • shamefest • show • Sillywood • skeezer • sour
star baggage • starrer • stretch • suit • talking head • tight
t • (to throw a) Rudin • toast • **track** • trackers • trades •
und • **vanilla extract** • vanity show • wank trade • wet
wheel • white label • with a bullet • with an anchor • **wrap** •
ty • against the law • Amazon • Ann O'Rexia • b-boys • bad
Baldwin • Barney • betty • beard • beast • **beer goggl**
e-yotch • bell hop • bender • **biddy** • biff • bim • bitch •
gnet • bod squad • boxmaster • bomber • bootie call • E
akdown • breeders • buffy • buppie • **cave bitch** • cha
eese kransky • chip trip • clock • clowns • cock block • c
radle robber • creep • dahmer • deeko • **dexter** • dick •
s wonder • dingleberry • doable • dog • double bagger • dc
• dork • dude • **dump the chump** • de facto • faggot •
• **farley** • fatzilla • filth • filthy • fine • fishing fleet •
cks • flock • fly girl • fox • freak • fugly • **full moon** • gal
• gal pal • **gaydar** • gettin' any? • good to his mom • gor
ot it going on • got skills • **granola** • halfing • hands off •
oe • helen keller • hen party • high maintenance • himbo • ho
/girl • homey clown • honey • **honey dripper** • hoodie • h
• hook in • **horkle** • hot ticket • hottie • in the club • I
ttison cargo • keeper • kick the ballistics • kleenex • lavend
and fleas • load • lowball • **mack daddy** • mack • mac
le • mad bitches • main squeeze • meat market • miss thir
et • mosquito bites • mudflaps • nasty • nasty lass • **nell**
rod • no-neck • **o-beast** • O.P.P. • our team • pash • pa
y bird • P.I.C. • pizza face • player • poindexter • poz •
-babe • pugly • puppies • **quimby** • ragamuffin • raspy •
cker • saucalicious • scab • scam • scene • **schwing** • sco
ot the gift • skank • skeezer • sketch • smooth daddy • snc
p on a rope • space vixen • spade a chick • spliced • spunl
uallie • square john • **squid** • stallion • star fucker • steady b
ep out • stunts • sweetie • tard • tasty • **tenderoni** • th
highs • tire kicker • **tomato** • trailer trash • tranzie • tro
bagger • umpa loompa • vacuumed • wang • walker • whi
• wigger • wilma • **winnie bago** • woman years • wuss
oo • yorkel • zootie • advertiser • beater • bed dancer • beer
e dyke • bird dog • blew-it • boney • **booted** • braille • b
et • broadie • **bust a left** • buy-n-die • caddie • California
ancer • candied • cashmere • cherry • croakwagon
chrocket • cruiser • derogs • detail • ding • dust 'em • fac

THE BODY BEAUTIFUL

Part I: Fashion

Fashion Forward

ballsack: a men's Speedo swimsuit. Also, a *banana hammock*.

BBB: a big beautiful woman—that is, one who wears "plus" sizes.

berber: a hairpiece. Also, *rug, shag, flying carpet, toup, headpaint*.

bionic: artifical or prosthetic. (Also see MORE SLAMS AND PROPS.)

buttfloss: a thong string bikini.

caesar: a style in which the hair is worn closely cropped, with bangs.

camel toe: extremely tight pants or leggings that show the outline of a woman's *coochie*.

(to go) coyote: to dress casually, as one would to visit the popular dive El Coyote. Not to be confused with *coyote trash*—people who visit the bar on a regular basis.

dap: stylish, *dapper*.

dazey dukes: extremely short cutoff shorts. From the *Dukes of Hazzard* character. Also, *daisy dukes* and *dukies*.

door knockers: oversized earrings.

fade: hairstyle in which the sides are very short or shaved, and the top is long, or if the wearer is African-American, sculpted into topiary. (Also see EVERYDAY LIFE.)

fashion forward: up on, or ahead of, the latest styles.

freeballin': describes a man sans underwear.

fried, died and swept aside: bleached, strawlike blond hair.

grips: tennis shoes. (Also see *grip*/EVERYDAY LIFE.)

jams: a type of long, baggy shorts for men.

jesus sandals: a type of heavy leather sandal for men or women.

kicks: shoes.

look: an ensemble that makes a statement, for better or worse: "So that top is a little short—it's a *look*."

lowriding: 1.) going beltless. 2.) wearing pants extremely low on the waist, a style that can lead to *construction worker crack, White boy crack, White boy butt, blue collar crack*.

(to) mack: 1.) to dress up. 2.) to dress or to be dressed in a way others find pimplike: "It was embarrassing—he showed up at my Dad's *fully macked out* in stacked heels and a leather coat." (Also see THE MEET MARKET and EVERYDAY LIFE.)

mackadacious: stylish, having great style and pizzazz.

over-the-shoulder boulder holder: a sports bra.

package: description of a man's crotch when he wears tight pants or shorts. Also *unit, sausage sling*.

PIBs: people in black. Art world hangers-on who may or may not dress entirely in black.

pleather: disparaging term for leatherlike vinyl. From *plastic* and *leather*.

pressed out: dressed up. Also, *mackin', macked out*.

profiling: conspicuously well dressed. Also, *styling and profiling*.

retail action: shopping: "Party tonight? Time for some serious *retail action*."

(to) sag: the art of wearing one's trousers very, very low.

sally ann: the Salvation Army thrift shop.

shades: sunglasses. Also, *bins, bics, gregories, peeps*.

sheepdog: a brassiere. Originally Australian. So called because it rounds them up and points them in the right direction.

(to) sport: to wear: "Check out Mark, he's *sportin'* a new goatee."

tackies: tennis shoes, sneakers. Also, *tennies, trainers, grips*.

threads: clothing.

wife beater: a man's sleeveless tank top, white or mesh, or any very tight man's T-shirt. Also, *muscle shirt*.

Part II: Improving on Nature

abs: abdominal muscles.

banana rolls: rolls of fat that peek from beneath one's bikini bottom.

bonus: breast implants. Also to *put on weight, rig, silicone carne, enhancement*. (Also see EVERYDAY LIFE.)

boxed: same as *buff*.

bro-patch: a tuft of hair grown at the tip of the chin.

buff: well-toned and muscled, tight. Also *cut, tight*.

burn: a chemical dermabrasion. Also, *peel, to get peeled:* "I can't get a facial this week, sweetie—I just got *peeled*."

Celia Cohen: a woman with breast implants. (from *silicone*.)

cut: *buff, tight*.

cut 'n' paste: plastic surgery: "When he hit the big 5-0, he knew it was time for a *cut 'n' paste* around the jawline."

enhancement: surgical enlargement.

rig rack uplift Celia Cohen

fakes: breast or pectoral implants. Also, *faked goods, phonies*.

flat tire: 1.) the result of a bad or uneven breast enhancement. 2.) any sagging breast.

fold: a slight sag of the breasts or rear end.

frankentits: enormous, surgically *enhanced* breasts. Used primarily in the adult film biz.

glutes: gluteus maximus, the primary muscles of the buttocks.

guns: arms, or more specifically, biceps. Also *tri's* (triceps) and *bi's* (biceps).

labret: a lip pierce.

lift: a surgical lift: *tittie lift, butt lift, neck lift*.

labret

mask: refers to the telltale tightness of a face that has undergone too many lifts. "Check the *mask* on what's–her–name over there—scary!" Also, *bad mask*.

Michael Jackson: a botched or obvious plastic surgery job.

nip and ship: in plastic surgery, a quick, easy outpatient procedure.

(to) pack the cracks: to get collagen injections.

pecs: pectoral muscles.

pebbles: a nubbly feeling under the skin caused by a buildup of lactic acid in the muscles, noticeable during massage.

plaster: silicone, or material used to enlarge a breast.

prince albert: a piercing through a man's urethra. Ouch!

puss 'n' boobs: a woman whose face and breasts have been enhanced by plastic surgery.

(to) put on weight: to get breast augmentations. Also, *honker help, hooter help,* and *swellin' melons.*

rack: large breasts, sometimes but not necessarily, fake: "Check the *rack* on that." Also: "*There's a crowd on her balcony.*"

rebuilt engine: a penis with an implant.

rig: 1.) enlarged breasts: "Nice *rig,* whaddit cost?" 2.) a man's *package.*

silicone-carne: breast enhancements.

skin job: plastic surgery.

tat: tattoo.

trainer: 1.) a personal fitness trainer. 2.) a cross-trainer, or multipurpose gym shoe.

uplift: surgery that uplifts, usually breasts or face. Also, *lift.*

yag laser: surgical laser used to remove tattoos.

yarmulke burn: that cute little bald spot on the back of many forty-something heads.

Part III: Getting Physical

beard: a veteran surfer, used with respect. (Also see THE MEET MARKET.)

benny: a novice surfer. Also, *grommet, barney.*

benny

big mama: the ocean.

Billy Hoyle: a geeky White basketball player.

blades: roller blades, or in-line skates. Also, *to blade.*

boardhead: a person obsessed by surfing.

break: a *tasty* surfing beach.

butt boarding: luging on a skateboard (instead of on a full-size luge board).

Casper: a person without a tan.

charger: an aggressive surfer.

(to) do damage: to excel, particularly at a sport: "She *does damage* every time she straps on her skis."

(to) draft: the dangerous but popular practice of bicycling so close behind a bus or truck that there is no wind resistance (and also, therefore, little time to stop).

fred: a novice bicyclist.

(to) gear up: to have appropriate equipment, clothing, or attitude: "I'm *geared up* for the win."

(to have great) handles: to be a good basketball dribbler.

hoople: a bicyclist who spends more time picking up expensive gadgets and accessories than he does riding.

hoops: the game of basketball.

hoopster: a basketball player.

localism: in surfing, the practice of giving outsiders *stink-eye* or worse.

macker: surferese for a wave that's too hard to handle.

pamela: a female lifeguard, particularly a very attractive one. Also, *pam*: "Check out the *pam* on the tower ramp." (from Pamela Lee/*Baywatch*).

(to) play hoops: to play basketball. Also, *shoot hoops*.

rager: a skater or surfer who does it well. Also, *to rage*.

(to) rip: to catch a big, scary wave.

road rash: caused by contact with cement while skating or *blading*.

rock: a basketball: "Pass me the *rock*."

'roid rage: a state of over-aggressiveness reputedly caused by steroids used to enhance athletic build or performance.

shirts and skins: a game of football, differentiating teams by either wearing shirts or going shirtless.

shred sled: a snowboard.

stabbin' cabin: a surfer van (from an archaic term for sex).

stick: a surfboard. (Also see *stick*/EVERYDAY LIFE.)

stink-eye: Originally what you gave somebody when he tried to encroach on your perfect *break*, just before you *keyed* the hell out of his car. Now any dirty look.

surfer's rash: 1.) a rash caused by pollution in the water. 2.) abrasions on the body caused by sand and rocks.

surf hamburger: what your body becomes if you don't jump off your Boogie board before it hits the shore.

tubular: originally described the shape of a perfect wave (for surfing), now means good, great, amazing.

two-planker: a person who uses traditional snow skis.

(to get) weeded: to take a particularly devastating fall. Also, *to get biffed, lunched, pounded, rooted, worked.*

yard sale: what happens when you fall skiing and your stuff goes all over the mountain.

WORK

I owe, I owe (so off to work I go)

(to give it the) ankle: to quit (as in, to walk). Also, to *take the ankle*: "I'll *take the ankle* before I'll take another pay cut."

assed out: 1.) over and done with. Also, *maxed out*, *played out*. 2.) broke.

(to give something) the axe: to fire a person or kill a project. Also, to give something *the bosh*.

backflips: what you do to impress a client.

baller: a very successful person, one with *juice*. Also, a *hard roller*.

bells and whistles: add-ons that make something (often, a project or contract) more desirable.

(to) bite: to copy, to plagiarize.

blind item: a small bit of business or celebrity gossip that runs in print either without naming the person or company it is about or without naming a source.

boffo biz: great business, business that's going gangbusters.

box: a computer monitor.

break: see *hit*.

BTW: by the way.

(to) bust (something): to promote, to pitch: "Tom's been *bustin'* that pitch all over town."

(to) bust a nut: 1.) to work hard. 2.) to close a deal.

(to) call a meeting: to announce one—that is, to be the person with the *juice* to require everyone's attendance.

chips and salsa: the inner workings of a computer: "It's not your software—there's a bug in your *chips and salsa*."

(to) circle the drain: describes a project that is near death.

civilian: anyone not in whatever business is being discussed.

client abuse: perpetrated *by* the client, not *upon* the client.

clone: that's a phone, not a sheep.

cojones: nerve, gall (Spanish for *balls*, but anyone can have 'em).

cold call: a potential customer who has never been *pitched* or contacted before. Also, *to cold call*.

comer: a highly motivated person on his or her way up (from *up and comer*).

(to) comp: to give free of *compensation*—usually in hopes of publicity or good word of mouth (similar to *to take care of*, which has less of a business connotation).

confab: a brainstorming session, a meeting (from *confabulation*).

crunch time: a business's busiest period, usually end of the year sales.

(to) data mine: to pull info off the Internet.

(to) decruit: to fire, downsize, layoff.

(to be) dialed in: (to be) well connected, in the know. Also *plugged in, connected, in the loop, hooked in, knows people*.

done deal: a *slam dunk*.

downtown: see *upmarket*.

drop dead: the deadline: "Just give me the *drop dead*."

(to) drop paper: to sign an agreement.

dump: a cocktail party or dinner fund-raiser.

(to) fish off the company pier: to date within your circle of coworkers.

flack: a personal publicist, or any press liaison (somewhat derogatory).

(to) flame: to attack via computer. Also, *flame mail, flame war.*

(to do a) flip: to do a turnaround, to change one's views, especially in a business context. (Also see *backflips.*)

(to) float: to *comp,* to give free of charge: "When you gonna *float* me a couple of CD's, my brother?"

fruit and nut run: what airline pilots call the flight to Los Angeles (sometimes San Francisco).

full nelson: a heavy pitch, a hard sell.

FYI: for your information.

garmento: person who works in the *rag trade.*

(to) gas: to promote, sell, hype.

gear head: this once meant any technically or mechanically inclined person, but now refers specifically to computer geeks. Also, *byte head, chip head, propeller head.*

glass tower vampire: entertainment lawyer or executive.

go: it's your turn, hurry up. Used in meetings to step up the pace: "Alice — marketing — *go!*"

(it's a) go: we've got clearance, it's going to happen. Also, *thumbs up.*

grind: 1.) the job. 2.) the same old routine. 3.) to hardsell. Also, the *jiz.* (Also see THE WHEEL MEANING.)

gweep: a person who works on a computer all day, a key puncher. Unlike a hacker, a *gweep* isn't doing it for fun.

GWP: *gift with purchase,* a promotion heavily used in the cosmetics retailing: "Clinique's got a great *GWP* lipstick at Nordstrom."

hanger appeal: the quality, in the *rag trade,* of being attractive on the rack: "That fabric is too slinky to have any *hanger appeal*—put it on a mannequin so the customers can see it." Sometimes crosses over to general usage: "Bill's a loser when you get to know him, but he's definitely got *hanger appeal.*"

(to play) hardball: to negotiate seriously (sometimes underhandedly).

(to be in) high cotton: to be doing well. Also, *tall corn.*

high maintenance: a client or any person who requires hand-holding. (Also see THE MEET MARKET.)

hit: 1.) in public relations, a TV or print mention of a client. 2.) the action of visiting a web site on the Internet.

huddle: a meeting, a *powwow.*

in the black: making a profit.

in the red: losing money.

in the velvet: making a quick, fat profit.

inning: a week.

in the black

jaboney: a real or self-proclaimed expert who's available anytime, anywhere, for a talk show appearance. Usually chosen as last minute backup. Also *press hound, press whore, press groupie.*

JC: Jewish credibility: to be, or to claim falsely to be, Jewish when that is perceived as helpful to career advancement: "She can't lose—she's bright, she's ambitious, and she's got *JC.*"

jiz: work, employment. Also, *juice.*

landline: a traditional phone line (as opposed to being on a cel phone). Also, *hardline.*

(on) life support: still in business, but barely.

light: attention, publicity, hype: "We gotta get that new album some *light.*" Also, *flash, noise, to be making noise.*

lock: a sure thing, a *done deal.* Also, *to have a lock on something:* "We wanted to rent that rehearsal space, but Randy's *got a lock on it* for the weekend." (Also see *locked/* STREETLIFE.)

(the) loop: what you're out of when you don't know what's going on.

loose cannon: an unreliable, unpredictable person or one who often puts his foot in his mouth (usually used in a business context).

loose cannon

mafia: any insider circle or powerful clique: the *Hollywood mafia,* the *rock mafia,* the *gay mafia,* which is also called the *velvet mafia.*

magalog: a mail-order catalogue disguised as a magazine.

Mc-: a prefix meaning cheesy, crummy, cheap, mindless: *McJob, McNewspaper, McFurniture* (from McDonald's).

meet and greet: an ostensibly social gathering whose real purpose is to promote networking.

mersh: art world term for clichéd, obvious, or sellout (from *commercial*). Also, *mershy.*

(to) milk it: to get as much as possible from a situation.

mommy track: that mythical slower track to professional success that allows women to devote time to home and children while continuing to work.

mouse potato: a person who whiles away hours on his or her computer (from *couch potato*).

mule: 1.) the electric car driven by postal workers. 2.) the (sometimes unwitting) person employed to move a package of drugs, usually by airplane.

(to) munge: to destroy—usually applies to computer files.

my girl: one's personal assistant, executive assistant, or administrative assistant. That is, what used to be called a secretary. Note that there are many male assistants, but they are not referred to as "my boy" (or as *my girl,* for that matter).

my people/your people: short for "have your people call my people," that is, "Now that we agree, let's let the underlings handle all the details." Also, *my peeps/your peeps.*

network dating: what used to be called *sleeping one's way to the top*—but now men can do it, too. Also *network whore*.

NSG: not so good.

(to be) on the same page: to be talking about the same thing, to be at least in rough agreement.

one sheet: a movie poster or ad, often stapled or glued to telephone poles and plywood walls at construction sites.

(to give the) O.O.: to give something the *once over*, a quick look. Also, an *eyeball*, a *look-see*.

out of the box: from the beginning.

outside the box: unusual, cutting edge.

paper chase: the quest to earn money and/or a degree.

pimp: a person with a lot of money and *juice* (in any line of work).

(to) play (someone): to manipulate, connive, or cheat someone—that is, *to play him for a fool*.

player: 1.) a creampuff, an easy client. 2.) a person who's willing to cooperate and negotiate (that is, a *team player*). 3.) an important person with a lot of *juice*. (Also see THE SCHMOOZEFEST, THE MEET MARKET, and STREETLIFE.)

P.O.P: point of purchase. Describes a product offered for sale near the cash register: "Those *elvis* pens weren't really moving until we put them *P.O.P.*"

power-: a prefix connoting a high degree of importance or relevance, as in a meeting with top executives at a *power lunch* or *power breakfast*. Also applies to any activity undertaken with vigor or enthusiasm: *power sweating, power workout*.

pow-wow: a business meeting, often impromptu.

pro-con: a publicist.

(to) push the envelope: originally from aerospace, referring to the *edge,* or limit, of the envelope of achievable speed. Now used to refer to any extreme: "That miniskirt is really *pushing the envelope* for a law firm."

rag trade: the clothing business.

(to) ride the boards: to drive around checking the condition of billboards after a *Santa Ana*.

'roids: Polaroid pictures.

roll: to bring on, to begin, as in *roll* calls or *roll* credits.

roll calls: to play back or to return recorded phone messages.

(to) roll over: to be an easy sale. Also, *roll over:* "I made fifty bucks before noon—my first *cold call* was a *roll over*."

schmata: clothing (used in the *rag trade*). Originally from Yiddish.

sexy: interesting, from a business perspective: "Pork bellies are looking *sexy* again."

shaker: what *comers* become when they make it (from *mover and shaker*).

(to) shit your own doorstep: to make a move that backfires. Also, *to soil your own nest*.

slam dunk: a sure thing.

(to be) slammed: to be overburdened with work: "Can't make it tonight, babe, I'm *slammed*." Also, *drowning, jammed, booked, buried, swamped*.

snail mail: that delivered by the Post Office as opposed to via E-mail.

(to) snipe: to staple or glue ads or *one sheets* to walls and telephone poles, usually by night.

SP: starting price.

spam: insipid, ubiquitous advertisements over the Internet.

(to) suck fumes: to be left behind: "Accept that transfer to Orange County, and you'll be *sucking fumes* for the next five years."

(to) tag: to appoint to a job: "She *tagged* Arthur for the deputy chief spot." (Also see STREETLIFE.)

(to) take: to have. One can *take* lunch (don't even suggest *doing* lunch) or *take* a meeting (*having* or *holding* meetings is passé), but if you can *call* one, you're *pissing with the big dogs*.

(to be) tasked: to be assigned work: "I'd like to chat, but they're *taskin'* me to go on a run."

taxpayer: a *civilian*, a person not in your business.

telephone number salary: one in the seven digits.

(to) tone: to sell photocopier toner (or, by extension, any product) by phone. Implies illegal or shady practices: "I'm looking for an agent, but for now, I'm still *toning.*"

topper: highest-ranking executive.

twofers: items that are two for the price of one.

Uncle Mo is on our side: auspices are favorable (from *momentum*).

upmarket: describes a product or service that is *upscale,* geared toward customers with money and taste. Also, *high end.* Also, *downmarket, downtown.*

vampire: a person who works the *vampire shift,* or graveyard shift.

veep: short for *vice president,* but sometimes applied to any executive.

wild posting: to plaster a building or construction site with posters and signs.

(to) wine/dine/sign: just what it sounds like.

zombie: a *vampire.*

be • bad version • bambino • bando • blow up • **bono** •
book • bootie record • box office • call sheet • cattle call •
a cha cha • chantoosie • ciao • **chopsocky** • churban • (
cock rock • craft • craft service • cut to the chase • deal me
velopment hell • DOA • drop • doughboy • films • flack
) flashing • go-see • goebbles • got ears • green room • gr
or rewrite • **helmer** • hickey • **high concept** • high **schm**
hit the streets • Hollywood • Hollywood heartbeat • horse bl
hyphenate • in the can • indie • indier than thou • Industry
jackets • jam • **japananimation** • juice • logline • (to le
AW • meatpuppet • ntbslt • offish • Oscar • Oscar nod •
er • Pasadena • peeled • pen • pitch • player • playola •
press whore • **product** • punch it up • Q • roll calls • sam
hmooze • shamefest • show • Sillywood • skeezer • sour
star baggage • starrer • stretch • suit • talking head • tight
t • (to throw a) Rudin • toast • **track** • trackers • trades •
und • **vanilla extract** • vanity show • wank trade • we
wheel • white label • with a bullet • with an anchor • **wrap** •
rty • against the law • Amazon • Ann O'Rexia • b-boys • bad
Baldwin • Barney • betty • beard • beast • **beer gogg**
e-yotch • bell hop • bender • **biddy** • biff • bim • bitch •
gnet • bod squad • boxmaster • bomber • bootie call •
eakdown • breeders • buffy • buppie • **cave bitch** • cha
eese kransky • chip trip • clock • clowns • cock block •
cradle robber • creep • dahmer • deeko • **dexter** • dick •
s wonder • dingleberry • doable • dog • double bagger • d
y • dork • dude • **dump the chump** • de facto • faggot
g • **farley** • fatzilla • filth • filthy • fine • fishing fleet •
icks • flock • fly girl • fox • freak • fugly • **full moon** • ga
• gal pal • **gaydar** • gettin' any? • good to his mom • go
got it going on • got skills • **granola** • halfing • hands off •
toe • helen keller • hen party • high maintenance • himbo • h
y/girl • homey clown • honey • **honey dripper** • hoodie •
t • hook in • **horkle** • hot ticket • hottie • in the club •
jettison cargo • keeper • kick the ballistics • kleenex • laven
e and fleas • load • lowball • **mack daddy** • mack • ma
ckle • mad bitches • main squeeze • meat market • miss th
onet • mosquito bites • mudflaps • nasty • nasty lass • **ne**
mrod • no-neck • **o-beast** • O.P.P. • our team • pash • p
rcy bird • P.I.C. • pizza face • player • poindexter • poz •
o-babe • pugly • puppies • **quimby** • ragamuffin • raspy •
rocker • saucalicious • scab • scam • scene • **schwing** • sc
oot the gift • skank • skeezer • sketch • smooth daddy • s
ap on a rope • space vixen • spade a chick • spliced • spu
squallie • square john • **squid** • stallion • star fucker • steady
step out • stunts • sweetie • tard • tasty • **tenderoni** •
r thighs • tire kicker • **tomato** • trailer trash • tranzie • t
o-bagger • umpa loompa • vacuumed • wang • walker • w
it • wigger • wilma • **winnie bago** • woman years • wu
hoo • yorkel • zootie • advertiser • beater • bed dancer • be
bike dyke • bird dog • blew-it • boney • **booted** • braille •
cket • broadie • **bust a left** • buy-n-die • caddie • Californ
cancer • candied • cashmere • cherry • croakwag
otchrocket • cruiser • derogs • detail • ding • dust 'em • fa

STREETLIFE

Romies, Roughnecks, and the 5-0

all day: a life sentence (prison lingo).

ambassador: a drug dealer who is not the main source.

angel dust: PCP. Also, *hog tranquilizer*.

bag 'em and tag 'em: directive to collect evidence or take a body away from the scene of a crime.

baller: a *player*, a *big pants*.

bang: 1.) heroin. 2.) to shoot up drugs. 3.) to shoot someone.

'banger: short for *gangbanger*. In general parlance, *banger* and *gangbanger* refer to any gang member, but on the street, the term often connotes one who is particularly violent.

(to) bank: 1.) to form a wall of people around a victim in order to mug him. 2.) to have or carry a lot of money.

barbie dolls: barbituates. Also, *barbies*.

(to get) bar coded: to be arrested.

barnyard pimp: a chicken dish (mostly prison lingo).

basehead: a crack addict, person who freebases. (Also see *basshead*/EVERYDAY LIFE.)

(to) beam up: to smoke crack or to get high. (Also see EVERYDAY LIFE.)

bid: a jail or prison sentence.

big pants: an important person, or one who thinks he is.

(the) big willy: a man who's on top, the boss, a *player*.

(the) bill: the set bail amount.

(to get) blisted: *to get booted, to get wasted* (from *bliss*, for marijuana).

blow: cocaine. Also, *perico, chibbles and bits, gack, yey–o*.

blue foot: a street hooker (originally British).

blunt: originally, a joint made by emptying out a Phillies Blunt cigar and stuffing it with pot. Now, any *fattie*.

(to) boast: to smoke pot: "Check out T, he's *boastin* the *Philly*."

(to) bomb: to concentrate heavily on a specific area in spray painting graffiti. (Also see *the bomb*/EVERYDAY LIFE.)

(to) boost: to steal, especially to shoplift. Also, *to pinch, to comack, to snake*.

(to get) booted: to get high. Also, *lit, baked, tweaked*. (Also see THE WHEEL MEANING OF LIFE.)

booya: the sound of a gun: "He walked right up to that chump and—*booya! booya!*"

bong juice: the smelly, potent water from a water pipe.

bottom: the underground, the underworld.

boulevard boys: male street hookers.

Brando: nickname for any high-powered hunting rifle.

(to be) buddhaed: to be stoned.

bumps: cocaine. Also, *blow, gack, yey-o, chibbles and bits, mi amigo, perico.*

(to) bust a cap: to shoot a gun, or to kill someone with a gun. Also, *to pop a cap.*

(to) bust a pipe: to smoke marijuana.

busted and dusted: arrested and processed—that is, fingerprinted and photographed.

bustin': to do drugs: "Larry's been *bustin' barbies* for the past week." Also, *sportin'*.

buttons: 1.) narcotic pills. 2.) peyote in its natural form, so called because it grows in buttons like mushrooms.

caddislacker: 1.) a shopping cart appropriated by a homeless person. 2.) a homeless person.

calico: a semiautomatic weapon.

cap: 1.) bullet. 2.) to kill: "Somebody needs *to cap* that *mofo!*"

(to do a) Carl Lewis: to flee the scene of a crime: "Cops never even saw him—he did a *Carl Lewis* and he was gone."

(to) carry: to carry a gun. Once specifically police lingo, now used by others.

(to) catch a pay: to be mugged.

(to) catch a wreck: to get beat up. Also, *to get served, to get punked.*

(to) chase the kettle: to get high.

(to) check: to murder. (Also see EVERYDAY LIFE.)

(to) chip: 1.) to do drugs occasionally. Usually, *chipping.* 2.) to work as a prostitute.

chirp: a quick hit of cocaine. Also, *gag, snort.*

(to be) chopped: to be high.

chrome: a handgun. Also, a *click.*

chronic: originally, really strong or chemical-treated pot. Now, any kind of marijuana. Usually, *the chronic.* Also, *bud, buddha, crab, ganj, herb, the kill, mota, the shit, the orange, KGB, method.*

clean: drug or alcohol free. (Also see EVERYDAY LIFE.)

(to) Clinton: to smoke *weed* without inhaling.

(to) clock: to sell drugs. (Also see EVERYDAY LIFE.)

Club Fed: Federal prison.

CMB: a petty thief, an opportunist (from *cash money boy*).

coast 'n' toast: a drive-by shooting.

cokie: a cocaine user, a coke head.

(to) come up: to steal.

cookies: crack-laced cigarettes.

coolie: a cigarette laced with cocaine (from Kool cigarettes).

cornelius: marijuana. Also, *bliss, dagga, dank, grifa, kanya, the kind* (for high grade), *lye, 1, mayo, one hitta quitta* (very potent stuff) *rope, sausables, schwag, tyrone, yesca, weed.*

crack: crack cocaine, that is, a form of cocaine that is smoked instead of sniffed or injected. Also, *breath of God, la roca* (Spanish for *the rock*).

crack house: a house in which crack is manufactured, distributed, and/or used.

crank: crystal methedrine. Also, *crystal, meth, hydro, glass.*

creedle: cocaine. Also, *blow, blips, devil's dandruff, flour, gerks, lady, nose candy. Flake, powder,* and *rock* refer to specific forms of the drug.

crip walk: a particular style of dancing practiced by hip-hop enthusiasts characterized by a low stance and outstretched arms (from the Crips gang).

(to) curb serve: to sell drugs on the street corner to clients in cars.

custies: drug customers.

derl: a derelict.

deuce: 1.) a drunk-driving charge. 2.) a two-dollar bill.

dickless tracy: a policewoman.

(to) dig for gold: to administer a urine test for drugs.

dime bag: the amount of cocaine you can get for ten dollars, which varies according to current market price. Also, *a dime*. The original meaning—the amount of *pot* you could buy for ten dollars—has been largely abandoned.

doobie: a marijuana joint. Also, *doob*.

dose me: please share your drugs.

DT: a detective.

duck: a squad car.

dump truck: an incompetent lawyer (prison slang).

eight-ball: 1.) an eighth ounce of cocaine. 2.) Old English 800 malt liquor.

elbow bender: an alcoholic.

(to) elmer: to get high by inhaling a gaseous substance from a bag.

epsom salts: the drug Ecstasy.

expiration date: time of death.

faded: 1.) drunk or high. Also, *schnackered, annihilated*. 2.) dead: "Joe's best *custie* got *faded*."

fattie: a fat joint. Also, *jiz, jinder, jizzoint, pinwheel*.

fattie

fed ex: an ex con.

fish tank: the area of a jail where suspects are held temporarily.

five-o: police officer, or a police car (from the cop show, *Hawaii Five-O*). Also, *bacon, berries, the heat, the fuzz, long johns, the man, popeye, roller, pigs, squirrels, squirrelies, one time.* Sometimes written *5–o*.

5140: to be intoxicated, from the police code books (pronounced fifty-one forty).

flamer: a handgun.

(to) flex: to try to intimidate with a show of force.

(to) fly Mexican airlines: to smoke marijuana. Also, *to fly Mexican air*.

(to be) folded: to be drunk. Also, *bent, pedo* (Spanish).

g: originally, a gangster or *gangbanger*. Now, any male. Also, *OG*, or *original gangster*, for *gs* over twenty-five.

gaffle: 1.) to arrest 2.) to steal, *to snake, to rook*. Usually used when something is stolen from you: "I got *rooked*."

gangster lean: this old favorite is back, and still means a style or stance practiced by gangsters.

gat: 1.) handgun. Also, *gak, heat, piece, roscoe, jammy, rod, steel.* 2.) to shoot or to kill a person.

gates man: a particularly brutal or fascistic cop (from former police chief Daryl Gates).

gauge: a shotgun or any gun.

(to) geeze: to shoot up.

(to) get Chinese: to get drunk or high.

ghetto bird: police helicopter.

giggle stick: a joint. Also, a *bammer.*

gimme: a handgun. Usually used by police officers and refers to the mugger's demand: "*Gimme* your money."

gladiator school: maximum-security prison. Also, a school for juvenile delinquents.

Glock: the brand name of a popular and powerful handgun.

goo ball: a brownie or any confection laced with *herb.*

green room: the gas chamber at San Quentin prison. (Also see THE SCHMOOZEFEST.)

gray goose: jail. Also, *pinta.*

green light: the go-ahead to attack any particular gang or opposing ethnic group: "The Crips have given the *green light* on any Bloods found in their path."

g-ride: being convicted for grand theft auto. (Also, see THE WHEEL MEANING OF LIFE.)

groin soccer: the process of physically subduing a suspect.

guzzler: an alcoholic. Also, *alkie, stewbum, elbow bender.*

(to) hang a jacket: to mark someone as a target of violence or retribution: "Stan better watch his back—Frank *hung a jacket on him.*"

hard candy: the target of retribution or revenge by a rival gang or enemy: "He *dropped a dime* on my brother. Now he's *hard candy!*"

hard rock: a seasoned criminal: "Don't fuck with him, he's a *hard rock roughneck.*" Also, *hard case.*

(to) hawk: to size up with the intent to steal: "They were dressed like cable repair guys, but I think they were *hawkin'* my *crib.*"

Henry: heroin. Also, *blue lady, china white, chinese rocks* (types of heroin), *chiva, doogie, horse* (generic terms).

herb: pot. Also, *herbal, herbals.*

hole in one: suicide, using a gun.

homo-sigh: a homicide detective.

hooch: a joint.

hoochie: 1.) a hooker. Also, *ho.* 2.) marijuana.

ho-stroll: the strip of Santa Monica Boulevard where hookers ply their trade.

house of D: The House of Detention.

(to be) housin': to carry a concealed weapon, or drugs.

(to) huff: to inhale an intoxicating substance (like glue) from a paper bag. Also see *elmer*.

hype: a person who shoots heroin.

ice: 1.) crack. 2.) diamonds. 3.) to kill: "Let's *ice* 'em." (Also see THE WHEEL MEANING OF LIFE and EVERYDAY LIFE.)

instant karma: *LSD*. Also, *blotter, blue cheer, blue sunshine, microdot* (for various types of LSD).

(to) jack: to steal, as in to *carjack*. Often by physical force.

jacket: criminal record. (Also see THE SCHMOOZEFEST.)

(to) jig: to stab a person with a knife.

johnnies: cops. Also, *chota, flamers, jake, jura, maria, po po, rollers,* 5–0.

joint: 1.) prison. 2.) a gun. 3.) a penis. 4.) adjective meaning the best: "That stuff is the *joint*." 5.) any artistic product — a film, a painting, an album. 6.) a bar or nightclub.

juicer: 1.) an alcoholic. 2.) a prostitute.

juvie: juvenile hall.

kalied: drunk or stoned.

KGB: marijuana (from *killer green bud*).

kite: prison lingo for a note passed secretly from inmate to inmate.

lead singer: a gang leader.

(to) lift: to steal.

(to get) lifted: to get high.

liquid heroin: Jagermeister liqueur.

liquid sky: heroin.

(to get) lit: to get high or drunk. Also, *to get baked, blasted, bombed, fucked up, hammered, henged* (from Stonehenge), *laced, lathered, lock-legged, looped, loopy, looted, lubricated, lushed, malty, pissed, plastered, shit-faced, tweaked, waxed, well-oiled,* and to get *nice, dumb,* or *stupid.*

loadie: person who uses drugs frequently. Also, *pothead, spleefer* (from *spleef,* or joint), *stoner, teahead, tweaker.*

(to be) locked: to be high on drugs: "I was *locked* on that *crystal* all night long."

locker: jail.

loud lucy: any potent alcoholic drink: "That's some *loud lucy!*"

lunatic soup: alcohol.

main course: patent medicines—that is, over-the-counter drugs.

the mamas and the papas: cop slang for a hard-core crime family.

(to) map the heavens: to spray paint graffitti on freeway overpass signs.

maserati: a homemade pipe for smoking drugs.

menu: one's constitutional rights. When a cop *shows the menu*, he is reading a suspect his Miranda warning.

(to be on a) meow: to be on a shoplifting spree.

Metro tux: a police term for gang wear, i.e., white T-shirt and pressed work pants.

miss greening: marijuana. Also, *moon cabbage*.

mook: a tough guy, a *bad ass*.

moon rock: heroin.

munchies: the state of hunger induced by smoking weed.

nic: nickel bag, or five dollars worth of cocaine.

nine: refers to either of two things a *g* might pull out of his pants: 1.) a nine-millimeter handgun. 2.) the proverbial nine inches.

(to) Nixon: 1.) to screw up a burglary or any job. 2.) to kill a person in a clumsy manner.

187: murder (from the police code book. Pronounced either one-eighty-seven, or one-eight-seven).

one-hit wheelchair bud: really strong pot.

on the muscle: a police term for an overly excited or nervous suspect.

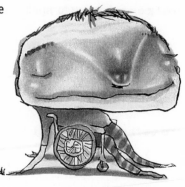

one-hit wheelchair bud

one time: a police officer (from the practice of passing a suspect once, then returning to hassle or arrest him).

oowop: an automatic machine gun. Also, a *streetsweeper*.

Oswald: affectionate term for a hunting rifle, named for Lee Harvey.

O.Z.: ounce of marijuana. Also, *a bag*.

(to) pack: to carry a gun. Often, *to pack heat*.

pan hassling: aggressive pan handling.

paper hanger: a person who knowingly writes bad checks.

papes: 1.) rolling papers. 2.) money.

player: 1.) a guy who's *living large*, making and spending money, enjoying the company of women. 2.) a pimp (mostly archaic). (Also see THE SCHMOOZEFEST, THE MEET MARKET, and WORK.)

pop: 1.) to shoot, as *to pop a cap*. 2.) to kill, usually with a gun: "He blinked, so they *popped* him." An older, less-used meaning is to punch: "I *popped* him on the chin."

(to) pop 'n' drop: to drink and drive.

pop fly: to kill a person by throwing him off a building.

(to get) popped: 1.) to be arrested or caught in the act. 2.) to be shot.

(to get) popped in bed: to be shot at close range.

porthole: a bullet wound, or bullet hole in an inanimate object.

primo: marijuana cigarette laced with cocaine. (Also see MORE SLAMS AND PROPS.)

product: drugs. Also, *godfather, poop, dynamite* (for very good drugs).

pruno: prison-made moonshine, usually made by fermenting bread, water, and fruit in a plastic bag.

(to) pull up: to challenge a person to a fight—that is, *to pull up*, or come close enough, to fight: "Why don't you *pull up, mofo,* and let's *dance!*" (originally, prison slang). Also, *to call someone out.*

racked: loaded with ammo: "The *gauge* is *racked.*"

radar: electronic ankle cuffs parolees wear so that their movements can be monitored. Also, *radar boots.*

rat boy: a cop killer.

red devils: a type of downers, or sedatives.

regulate: a prison term for punishment or severe beating.

retailer: a drug dealer.

roachie: rophynol, or the date rape drug. From the brand name *Roche*. Also, *ralphies, roofies.*

road kill: a person who has been killed by an automobile—especially, run over on purpose. Also, *flapjack, frisbee.*

(to have a) rocket in the pocket: to be armed. Also, *mauser in the trouser.*

romie: a person who uses drugs.

roughneck: a young man—especially a streetwise, tough, bad-ass.

'round the way: 1.) the neighborhood: "He's from *'round the way.*" 2.) down to earth, not pretentious: "She's a *'round the way* girl."

rush flux: detox—the process of detoxifying from drugs and/or alcohol.

scoop: the hypnotic drug *GHB*, also called *cherry meth* and *liquid X.*

second-story work: breaking and entering. Also, *B and E.*

shank: a knife, particularly a homemade or prison-made knife.

sheep dip: a weak drink.

sherm: peyote. Also, *magic mushrooms, shrooms.*

shottie: a shotgun. Also, *thumper pumper.*

skag: heroin. Also, *china white, h, horse, sweet lady jane.*

(to) skeeze: to shoot cocaine or heroin.

(to) slam: to shoot up, that is, to inject an illegal drug. Also, *to geeze*.

(to) smoke: to murder. Also, *to off, take out, whack,* or *wax*.

spacebar: *crack* and *angel dust* rolled into a cigarette.

(to) steam: to overwhelm a victim with a huge show of force. Also, *steamers* for gang members.

step on: to cut cocaine or any powdered drug with a lesser substance.

stoner: a person who smokes marijuana. Note that *stoner chicks* are those who hang with *stoners*, whether or not they smoke themselves.

(to be) strapped: 1.) to be carrying a gun. 2.) to be holding drugs. Also, *housin'*, *packing*. (Also see EVERYDAY LIFE.)

street: credible. Also, *to have street credentials*.

supermax: maximum-security prison.

sweet lucy: any cheap wine.

swervin' mervin: a drunk driver.

tag: 1.) graffiti artist's stylized name. 2.) to mark with graffiti.

tag crew: a gang or group that *tags* together. Also, *tag team*.

tagger: a graffiti artist.

t-bone: overtime pay. Used primarily by jailors.

Thomas Wolfe: a life sentence (from *You Can't Go Home Again*).

(to) throw signs: to make hand signals showing gang affiliation.

(to) throw up: to mark one's *tag*.

tommy gun: a hypodermic needle.

transvestite: an undercover cop.

trim: 1.) to pick a lock. 2.) sex: "I gotta get some *trim*."

tweaker: a drug user.

2-5: a 25-millimeter handgun.

(to) urban surf: to ride atop a moving car.

utensil: a pipe or roach clip.

veterano: a seasoned gangster (from the Spanish). Also, *OG*.

(to) vick: to rob, to mug.

vitamins: drugs of various types: *A* (LSD, from acid), *C* (cocaine), *E* (ecstasy), *T* (marijuana, from tea).

(to) waste: to kill.

(to be) wasted: to be stoned.

weight: a package of drugs. Also, a *fold* for the folded paper square used to carry cocaine or other powdered drugs. (Also see EVERYDAY LIFE.)

(to be) whipped: to be addicted (from *pussywhipped*). (Also see EVERYDAY LIFE.)

whirlpool: a crime in which a group of boys surround a girl (originally in a swimming pool), molest her, and move quickly to the next victim.

(to) wild: 1.) to go on a group crime spree. 2.) to make more benign mischief, running wild.

writer: a graffiti artist. Also, *tagger*.

yard bird: a con, a prison inmate.

yard dog: a liar.

yo-yo: person who commits suicide by hanging.

zepplin: a joint.

zonables: joints, something to get *zoned* on.

zooted: drunk. Also, *to be sailing*.